BARRY JACKSON
AND THE
LONDON THEATRE

Barry Jackson, from a Drawing
by
Dame Laura Knight, A.R.A.

BARRY JACKSON

AND THE

LONDON THEATRE

By G. W. Bishop

With a Foreword by Charles B. Cochran
Illustrations from the Designs of
Paul Shelving

BENJAMIN BLOM  New York/London

133|97

First Published 1933
Reissued 1969 by
Benjamin Blom, Inc., Bronx, New York 10452
and 56 Doughty Street, London, W.C. 1

Library of Congress Catalog Card Number 76-81972

Printed in the United States of America

*To all the actors and actresses who have
appeared under the Barry Jackson banner*

AUTHOR'S NOTE

WHEN the suggestion was first made that there should be a record of Barry Jackson's ten years' work in the London theatre I discussed the matter with Bernard Shaw. He agreed so emphatically that I knew I could call on him for help and advice. He has given both, and, in addition, made some valuable corrections on the proofs, for all of which I have to thank him. I am also grateful for the permission to print the letters and other Shaw material that enliven many of the chapters.

My gratitude is equally due to Cyril Phillips, H. K. Ayliff, Nancy Leverton, William Jermy, and other members of Barry Jackson's staff for the great assistance they have given me. Without their help the book could not have been written.

G. W. B.

CONTENTS

CONTENTS

viii

LIST OF ILLUSTRATIONS

FOREWORD

by

CHARLES B. COCHRAN

THIS book is a record of achievement in the theatre unequalled by any other manager since the War. Sir Barry Jackson is England's great man of the theatre. His influence on the Drama of his time cannot be appraised too highly.

Few people imagined, when Barry Jackson opened his little experimental Repertory Theatre in Birmingham, that his activities would ever have so profound an effect on our national theatre. Since he began active work in London, bringing to us by way of Birmingham and Malvern new plays, new actors, and new ideas, he has been the Fairy Godmother of the British Drama in the West End.

That he should think of retiring from management, as is hinted in the postscript to Mr. Bishop's book, is unthinkable. He cannot be spared.

I can well understand the mood in which the man who loves the theatre for its own sake determines to " chuck the whole thing." Sometimes financial losses and artistic disappointments are all one can show at the end of a long spell of arduous labour and high endeavour. But Sir Barry is too high-mettled an adventurer in the theatre to be cast down for long, and I look forward with confidence and hope to the great work that he, with his culture, knowledge, sincerity, and enthusiasm, has still to give us.

I must, however, join a friendly lance with Sir Barry when he concludes that West-End theatres cannot be made to pay with good plays, and instances the financial losses which his policy has brought him.

I cannot regard these losses as a convincing argument by themselves, nor can I accept Mr. Shaw's conclusion that if a play taking as much as £1,000 a week cannot be made to pay, the theatre in the West End cannot flourish unless it is subsidised by the Government.

In the West End of London a thousand pounds taken in eight perform-ances is not a very large sum and certainly does not, to my way of thinking, show any very eager demand by any large part of the public to see the play. I fancy a great deal more than £1,000 a week was paid to see Mr. Shaw's *Saint Joan*, for which a large and very real public demand did exist.

People did not rush so readily to see Mr. Shaw's *Too True to be Good*, but is it as good a play? I think it is pretty generally admitted that, in spite of its many merits, it is not.

Its failure must not be exclusively blamed on the West-End public. I have not heard of its being successful in America or elsewhere, whereas *Saint Joan* drew crowded houses wherever, and in whatever language, it was played.

It is only real outstanding successes that can expect to make money in the theatre to-day. There is no midway. Which is good for the standards of the theatre.

Practically the same applies to Mr. Somerset Maugham's recent play, *For Services Rendered*, which the public does not appear to have so far supported as enthusiastically as most of the critics' notices would have led one to expect. Is it really so good a play, and is it one that could be expected to make money? It is not that the public is necessarily afraid of the " hard bitter realism " of the play, for I venture to suggest that it is no more a realistic play than Sean O'Casey's *The Silver Tassie*. Mr. Maugham's characters and situations are not realistic, but invented to drive home his theories concerning the post-war world, and I fancy the public instinctively feels that they do not ring quite true. Judged by the highest standards—artistic rather than box-office—*For Services Rendered* is not " the Master " at his best.

xii

Why did Sir Barry have only one year showing a profit, as we are told, and that a very small one? We are given one reason. The profitable plays, including such outstanding successes as *The Farmer's Wife* and *The Barretts of Wimpole Street,* had to bear the very heavy administrative expenses of a theatrical organisation maintaining " so many necessary responsible employees on the permanent staff."

Far be it from me to compare my work in the theatre with that of Sir Barry, but I may be permitted to say this.

My accountants have recently certified that my productions between May 1927 and October 1932 have made a net profit of £143,246.

My permanent organisation consists of one General Manager, one General Stage Director, Miss Elsie April to help me with my music, Miss Cissie Sewell to see that my dancers do not slack, a secretary, two shorthand-typists, a telephone girl, an office boy, and myself.

It may be that Sir Barry has been too much the Fairy Godmother of the theatre and not an actual day-by-day worker in the theatre. To carry on with so small a staff, I have to work sixteen hours a day most days of the year. That's the theatre. Yet I generally control actively and personally two or three simultaneous productions in the West End, besides my interest in tours in the provinces, productions in America, and a host of other activities in London and elsewhere.

Again, it may be that Sir Barry has limited himself too narrowly in his choice of material. It may be that the theatre can only flourish on a variety of fare, and that there can be as much art in a revue as in a play by Shaw or Maugham.

A successful revue might have offset the losses on *Too True to be Good.*

In actual practice not all my profits have been made by the lightest forms of entertainment nor all my losses from aiming high. I lost £15,000 on *The Miracle,* but I have also lost £15,000 on a revue.

There will always be these ups and downs, but my own experience leads me to affirm this: by continually aiming at the very best one can do over the whole field of the theatre, and by giving the ship its ha'p'orth of tar, but not two pennyworth if a ha'p'orth will do, the West-End theatre business can be profitable, and that too with plays of a standard which is improving every year.

In conclusion, I should like to pay tribute to Mr. G. W. Bishop, whose industry and enthusiasm have produced this valuable record of great theatrical achievements. Mr. Bishop is well known as probably the best-informed writer on theatrical matters in this country. His keen interest in plays and players, his love of the drama in all its forms, his untiring quest for information, have added the present fascinating and reliable commentary to the debt which the profession and the public already owe him as a journalist.

CHAPTER I

A MAN OF THE THEATRE—THE BEGINNINGS—BERNARD SHAW'S ADVICE

IT is only within the last year or two that Barry Jackson has permitted his name to appear on the advertisements of his productions in London. Previously the bills announced that the Birmingham Repertory Company would present such and such a play. It was a cumbersome designation which had ceased to have any meaning. Although he has remained director and still takes an active interest in the work at Birmingham, for many years the Repertory Theatre has been conducted with its own producer and a separate company, which has on rare occasions only been seen in London.

This modesty on the part of Barry Jackson has been in an important sense a mistake. A name is a trade-mark in the theatre that is all the more necessary when the manager is no longer an actor. It provides personality and crystallises the quality of the entertainment, particularly when the word repertory is associated in the London mind with Lancashire kitchens, the Ireland of Synge and Lady Gregory, and the fairyland of Gilbert and Sullivan. If his work in London had been done in one theatre, which was thus associated with a definite policy, the nomenclature would have mattered less, but the interest has been dissipated because the productions have been given at the Regent, the Court, the Kingsway, the Queen's, and a number of other theatres.

The record in this volume will do something to focus the attention on ten years of fine endeavour. It is a story of experiment, of a good deal of achievement and a certain amount of failure, with the ups-and-downs of fortune that followed any attempts to raise the level of the post-war theatre. Many artists have their share in the work, but, in the main, it is the story of a man of wealth and taste who was prepared to subsidise the theatre with his time and money so that he could share his pleasures with other people. In every other country in the world—"except Peru," as Miss Horniman used to say—the theatre is recognised as a national institution, satisfying an elemental and universal human need, and is subsidised by the State. Through the ages it has been supported by Church, Emperor, or wealthy patron, and it is possible to date its degeneracy from the time it was expected to make profits, not for artists, but for individuals whose interest in the theatre was purely as an investment. During the war a great deal of money was made in third- and fourth-rate entertainments, and we are now suffering from this financial aberration in high rents and inflated salaries.

Of course, it would be foolish to maintain that the theatre should not pay, although, paradoxically, it is becoming increasingly true that the theatre conducted with the sole object of making profits is not very likely to do so. The theatre is an art with a curious tradition of glory and squalor behind it, but if it is to pay at all it must be run by artists : it is the plays that no business man would expect to make money that often run for months and years.

Not that Barry Jackson has made money in the theatre. He has, on the contrary, lost a very great deal, for the reason that the profits on the productions like *The Farmer's Wife*, *The Apple Cart*, and *The Barretts of Wimpole Street* have been spent in experimental seasons at other theatres, in expensive tours to Canada, and in running the Birmingham Repertory Theatre and the annual Malvern Festival. It must be remembered that he entered into London management four years after the end of the war, and he and one or two other people with enlightened ideas have had to clear up the mess left by the commercial managers. It has been uphill work, and a comparison of the plays that succeed to-day and those which were popular in 1916–1918 will indicate the improvement in the public taste. This record will show that Barry Jackson has had his share in the pioneer work. The plays produced (with occasional exceptions) have been pieces that demanded

2

to be presented by their intrinsic merit, and they have ranged from Bernard Shaw's metabiological pentateuch *Back to Methuselah* to Harold Chapin's diaphanous little comedy, *The New Morality*; from *Hamlet* in modern costume to *Harold* in fancy dress. The selection has been catholic, and has ranged from the mediævalism of *Saint Bernard* to the formalities of expressionism, from Ibsen to Rutland Boughton, from realism to fantasy.

It is characteristic of Barry Jackson that whenever he talks about his theatrical projects he always refers to " our " and not " my " work. He has had the splendid co-operation of so fine a producer as H. K. Ayliff, such a great theatre designer as Paul Shelving, and a company that has produced Cedric Hardwicke and Gwen Ffrangcon-Davies—two of the best actors on the English-speaking stage. The work owes a great deal to these artists, and, on the other hand, they owe almost everything to Barry Jackson who gave them the opportunities. They might have made their mark in the theatre —or they might not ! Cedric Hardwicke might now be carrying on his father's medical practice, and it is possible to conceive that Gwen Ffrangcon-Davies would be earning a precarious living as a singer, or that Ayliff would have remained an actor instead of becoming a prominent producer. This is idle conjecture, and it would be as futile to ask what Barry Jackson would have made of his life if, like the young lady in *Heartbreak House*, he had not had a love of Shakespeare implanted in him at a very early age by his father.

Barry Jackson's earliest memory is the sight of a pantomime head being thrust out of the window of his home in Birmingham. Theatricals played an important part in the household, and birthdays were always celebrated by the performance of a home-made play or pantomime usually written by his father, members of the family being responsible for the scenery and costumes. Recently he came across a programme of *Dick Whittington and his Cat* which was performed on January 1, 1877—two years before he was born—and it is interesting to note that Dick Whittington was played by his sister, Minnie Jackson, the mother of Cecily Byrne. One of his earliest photographs

3

was taken by his father with a drop curtain as a background, and many of his boyhood associations have to do with the family theatricals. If this book were a life of Barry Jackson rather than the story of his work in London it would be fascinating to trace the origin of his father's interest in play-acting. None of George Jackson's ancestors appears to have had anything to do with the theatre. His father—Barry Jackson's grandfather—was an engineering contractor with a considerable business, and so stern and implacable a parent (indeed, he seems to have resembled Edward Moulton Barrett) that the son ran away from home at the age of fourteen and took a situation with a grocer in Birmingham. A few years later he was able to set up in business, and when Barry Jackson was born—the youngest child by ten years—his father had made a considerable fortune and was able to enjoy a certain amount of leisure. He devoted a great deal of time to the boy, whose chief pleasure was to listen to the plays of Shakespeare being read out of the Staunton Edition, with the John Gilbert illustrations.

This was Barry Jackson's education. True, he went to a preparatory school for a time, and afterwards had a tutor, a man of great intelligence and wide knowledge who interested him in poetry and astronomy and the things that are not taught in academies. At the age of sixteen he was sent to Geneva to polish up his languages. Then he was articled to an architect in Birmingham and, although he loathed the office and spent much of his time, not in drawing plans, but writing plays and designing scenery for his amateur productions, he realises now that the training has been of extreme value in the theatre. He never practised as an architect, and left the office when he was in his early twenties. The father, then a partial invalid, was willing to allow his son to work out a career in his own way, and Barry Jackson turned naturally to the theatre. The genesis of the Birmingham Repertory Theatre can be found in the dining-room of The Grange, their house on the outskirts of Birmingham, where Foote's comedy, *The Lyar*, was presented in 1903. A series of amateur productions—either of original plays written by Barry

4

Jackson or forgotten pieces found in Dodsley's *Old Plays*—followed, until *The Interlude of Youth* in 1907 was repeated in a mission hall in Birmingham, thus leading to the formation of the Pilgrim Players and in February 1913 to the opening of the Birmingham Repertory Theatre.

Barry Jackson is in a very thorough sense a man of the theatre. His own talents have been kept in the background, for, from the beginning, he has been keener on getting other people to act than on acting himself, but in the early days he played a number of parts. In addition he has written plays, produced them, arranged the music for some of the productions, designed and painted the scenery, and made costumes. He directed the production of *The Immortal Hour* and, although it was not attributed to him, he was mainly responsible for the settings of one of the recent plays at the Queen's. If people imagine that he is a wealthy dilettante with the theatre as a hobby they are entirely mistaken. Is there any other manager in the West End of London who can claim his qualifications? He reads a great many of the plays that are submitted, the final choice being made by him, and young authors who show promise in play-writing are seen and encouraged.

Nor is his interest confined to his own ventures. He believes that the future of the theatre is to a great extent in the hands of the amateurs and the community players all over the country, and he spends a good deal of time in lecturing in Little Theatres, not only in this country but in Canada. He has paid two visits to the Dominion, where it would not be an exaggeration to say that the revival of interest in the theatre—which has been nearly strangled by the invasion of American film magnates—is partly due to his efforts. The Malvern Festival (for which a big company rehearses for two months) is conducted on such a scale that it can never hope to pay. He throws himself whole-heartedly into this annual event—which attracts visitors from all over the world—because it is another means of focussing attention on the theatre.

It is a case of a life that has been dedicated to the drama, and Barry Jackson's " call " to the theatre would appear to have been as real as another man's

5

" call " to religion. There is indeed something that is akin to religious fanaticism in his outlook. He has, in occasional moments of despair, threat-ened to give it all up (in fact, he tried to do so for a few months at Birmingham) and spend his time as many people in his position spend their time. He has wanted for the last thirty years to take a yacht and visit the lesser-known islands in the South Seas. He could easily afford to do so, but he will probably never get there, although he manages every now and then to slip off for ten days and walk across the Welsh Hills, a treat to follow the strenuous social weeks of the Malvern Festival. His recreations, according to *Who's Who in the Theatre*, are given as " travelling and painting," and he indulges in both : travelling about the country giving lectures on various aspects of the theatre and painting scenery for his productions.

He dislikes the frothy round of social life usually associated with the theatre, and is seen as rarely as possible at cocktail parties, Sunday night dinners, or grill-room suppers. He is a strange paradoxical creature, for in many ways he is the last person you would expect to find running a West-End theatre ; he lives very simply and likes to be in bed early. When he can get away, he is to be found pottering about the garden of his small house on the top of the Malvern Hills—trying to get flowers to grow in a particularly bad bit of soil. It is characteristic that he has managed to secure Allardyce Nicoll as a week-end neighbour, and the Sunday evenings in the country are spent in discussing old plays and talking over plans for the future.

Gardening is a good recreation for a theatre manager, for a gardener is a hopeful person in perpetual struggle with things on, under, and above the earth. Only by sheer grit and determination does he manage to grow fine flowers, and he optimistically thinks that next year will be a better season. The good gardener does not look backward but forward.

It is Barry Jackson's dream of an ideal theatre with a pit extending to the footlights, cheap prices for all the seats, a permanent company of enthusiastic players and a constant change of plays, that keeps him going. Almost against his will he has had to accept the ordinary conditions in the West End of London—the big shop-window and long runs that are to make money for Malvern and Birmingham and Canadian tours. Nevertheless he has his moments of depression. There was one in the June of 1928, when he felt thoroughly disheartened about his ventures and wrote to Bernard Shaw, who has been for some years his friend and confidant. In the course of his long letter he said:

" I enclose a list of plays for which I have been responsible in London since 1918. Every production has lost money in varying sums from £10,000 downwards. The only plays which have paid their way are the two works of Eden Phillpotts and John Drinkwater's *Abraham Lincoln,* and it took me three months of solid loss to induce the public to come to one of these. Where are we who love the theatre, and are of sincere endeavour, situate ? Is history going on repeating itself to the end of time, and is the Birmingham Repertory Theatre to go the way of the Horniman and Barker ventures ?

" The financial loss, as you see, has been no light burden to fall on the shoulders of one individual. But quite apart from this is the more important fact of the moral effect on the public and the members of my staff. Many of the latter who are with me for a transitory period perhaps care only for treasury night, but I refuse to believe they are in the majority.

" The causes of our troubles are legion. To take a few: the theatre is absolutely permeated with purely financial interests; the new rich will not go to intelligent plays (one might include many of the older rich), and un-fortunately we depend upon them for a part of our income, and when they do come, they often are a nuisance to everybody and themselves; the cheaper seats are so uncomfortable that I wonder anyone sits upon them; then we have the difficulties of advertising (which to-day appears to be the only method of inducing anyone to do anything); and the fact that in London we are living in furnished apartments, so to speak, with no roof of our own."

7

He asked G. B. S. for his advice, and a few days later he received the following reply:

"MY DEAR BARRY JACKSON,

"In reply to your important letter of the 8th I have really nothing to say that you do not know already. Except that the situation has been worsened by an inflation of theatre rents and the rise in salaries and prices of all sorts through the war it remains much as it has been throughout my experience, which began with Grein's Independent Theatre, the Stage Society, and Miss Horniman's start at the old Avenue Theatre in 1894, when *Arms and the Man* was produced by her. But none of these effected a lodgment as a going concern in London; and nothing that has any bearing on your present position happened until 1904, when Vedrenne and Barker started at the Court Theatre with the unrepeatable asset of a tame author (myself) carrying a reserve of unacted plays at the back of his current activities, and a beautiful young genius—actor, author, and producer of exquisite taste—as partner in the concern. There was no capital: the venture paid its way and yielded to the two partners, not always the thousand a year apiece they put themselves down for, but near enough to it to keep them going for a few years. But Barker was bent on a real repertory theatre (this was never realised) as distinguished from a short-run theatre; and both he and Vedrenne wanted to launch out into a real West-End theatre. I believed in the fixed short-run system, and not in the nightly-change repertory system except as a remote development of the fixed short run; and I greatly doubted whether the enterprise would bear expansion; but I agreed that we could find out the limit only by going on until we were stopped.

"Well, we went on until we were stopped; and the winding-up cost Barker every rap he had, and I had to disgorge a sum which may have been equal to all the royalties I had taken, or may not: I never made the calculation; but it was a substantial sum, anyhow.

8

" On the basis of our experience Barker calculated that a self-supporting repertory theatre was impossible ; but that with a theatre free of rent and rates he could do it. That meant a municipal theatre.

" After that Lord Howard de Walden backed Barker in a lordly way at the St. James's and lost. He afterwards, at my request (' Will you put down £500 if I do the same ?') backed him in a small way at the Little and Kingsway Theatres, and did well out of it through the success of *The Great Adventure*. Finally came the war and Barker's retirement on his second marriage. Nothing occurred meanwhile to shake his calculation that a highbrow theatre could not exist without an endowment sufficient to cover at least rent, rates, and taxes.

" Then you took up the running, with, as it seems to me, virtually the same moral : that is to say, an enthusiast with an independent income could run a repertory theatre in a provincial city for no more (barring his own labour) than it would cost to run a steam yacht. My guess as to Miss Horniman is that her experience came to the same thing.

" Now it is hardly possible for a private person to stand this racket without getting cold feet when the adventure has lost its first novelty and exhausted its possibilities of further novelty without any sign of becoming a big national institution. Also one gets tired of the discouragement of the critics, who soon become most generous in their recognition of last year's work, but invariably praise it only to show what a terrible falling off there is this year. My last play but one is always a masterpiece : my last play is always most unsatisfactory ; and this holds good also of the manager's productions.

" Every year almost, no matter what you deal in, the cost of selling the article becomes greater in proportion to the cost of producing it. Unless you shout, Buy, buy, buy from the walls and newspaper columns and railway stations louder than your competitors you are overlooked.

" Nevertheless, I am not convinced that with capital enough a much nearer approach to solvency, and certainly a great saving of business worry in hiring theatres, might not be achieved.   The first thing to do is to give up once for all the snobbery of the West-End box office and face the fact that good drama must live by the class that cannot afford more for an evening's entertainment than five shillings first class, half a crown second class, and a shilling third class.   The rich people must be thrown over completely, not because they are less susceptible than the relatively poor to dramatic art, but because they can afford to pay for so many counter-attractions both at home and in society, whereas the shilling and half-crown people have to choose between a theatre and a dull evening in a not too comfortable home.   Even the present shilling galleries are better fun than the domestic alternative.

" But low prices will not pay in small theatres.   When the Bancrofts introduced the tiny theatre and the cup-and-saucer drama, they had to intro-duce ten-shilling stalls and abolish the pit, which until then came right up to the orchestra and was the heart of the house.   By doing so they smashed your theatre and mine and produced the present impasse.

" Therefore we need large theatres ; and a large theatre in a central situation in London means a huge ground-rent, with a correspondingly high valuation and heavy rates.   It may be therefore that a central theatre would be im-possible without a free site and an exemption from rates as an educational institution.   But in the suburbs or in the provinces large theatres, moderate prices, and morning dress might make the manager's situation, if not eligible, at least bearable.   Finally, the municipality might take it on if there had been sufficient propaganda of the municipal idea to make that step popular and possible—if only to enable the dole system to reach its historic climax in bread and circuses.

" What to suggest is not so clear.   The Old Vic has kept afloat with all sorts of odd scraps of endowment and sending the hat round, trading heavily on Shakespeare's sanctity, but making its money by Opera.   Incidentally it is squeezing all the money that is to be got out of the public for Sadler's Wells, whilst the Stratford people are draining the Americans.

10

" Neither of them has asked for a subsidy, though both would if they thought they had a chance of getting it. The question is, What are you to ask for or propose if you go beyond a mere statement of the situation ?

" Meanwhile, the old Shakespeare Memorial Theatre Committee is sitting helplessly on the £70,000 put down by Carl Meyer. They helped Archie Flower to finance Bridges Adams's Stratford Company with the interest; but now the Charity Commissioners will not allow them to do anything with either the principal or interest except build a National Shakespeare Theatre in London at a cost which will remain beyond their means until the £70,000 has accumulated at compound interest to half a million, the date of which event may be fixed roughly at 1970 ! The utter refusal of the British public to contribute anything to hasten the process, and the fact that practically the entire principal was put down by a German, makes the national part of the business such a hollow sham that one could very well call on the Charity Commissioners to make a new scheme. But if you ask me what scheme, I am stumped. Between private adventurers like yourself and State and municipal theatres it is not easy to find a *tertium quid*.

" And then the films—the talking films and their future !

" It is no use : I give it up.

" Ever,
" G. B. S."

It was really G. B. S. who saved the situation. The following year he offered Barry Jackson the first refusal of *The Apple Cart*, and took an active interest in the Malvern Festival at which the play was first produced in this country. *The Apple Cart* ran successfully at the Queen's for nine months, and it was followed by the even longer run of *The Barretts of Wimpole Street*.

CHAPTER II

"ABRAHAM LINCOLN"—BRINGING "THE IMMORTAL HOUR" TO LONDON
—OTHER PRODUCTIONS AT THE REGENT

ALTHOUGH this book is a history of the first ten years of Barry Jackson's work in the London theatre, starting with *The Immortal Hour* which opened on October 13, 1922, a reference should be made at the outset to *Abraham Lincoln*, which Nigel Playfair brought to London in February 1919. He has already told the story of that fine adventure in his entertaining book on the Lyric Theatre, Hammersmith. John Drinkwater's connection with the Birmingham Repertory Theatre goes back to 1904, when a group of players gave occasional performances in the dining-room of The Grange. A programme of *Twelfth Night* exists showing that Fabian and Feste were taken by John Drinkwater and Barry Jackson. When the Pilgrim Players were formed in 1907 Drinkwater was one of the founders, later becoming producer and general manager of the Birmingham Repertory Theatre which was opened in 1913. While he was there he acted over sixty parts and also wrote a number of short plays, in one of which, *Ser Taldo's Bride*, he collaborated with Barry Jackson.

Abraham Lincoln was Drinkwater's second full-length play. It was produced on October 12, 1918, a few weeks before the end of the war, and the popular imagination was caught at once. The Birmingham Repertory Theatre was filled for a month, and the piece was revived within three weeks. Early in 1919 Nigel Playfair was looking for a play for the little theatre which he had just acquired at Hammersmith, and someone gave him a copy of *Abraham Lincoln* by a practically unknown author. Although he recognised its merits he was dubious whether a biographical play with verse

13

choruses would be likely to put the Lyric on its feet; and anxious to watch the effect on the audience, he made a journey to Birmingham to see it acted. Before he left he offered to present the company on sharing terms at Hammersmith.

Nigel Playfair would be the first to admit that it was *Abraham Lincoln* and the Birmingham Repertory Company that placed the Lyric, Hammersmith, on the theatrical map of London. The first-night audience was enthusiastic, there were excellent notices in the press next day, but like other successes with which Barry Jackson has been associated, it was some time before the public discovered the play. During the first few weeks business was very bad. But people began to talk, William J. Rea's fine performance as Lincoln attracted increasing attention, and Hammersmith became a place of pilgrimage. *Abraham Lincoln* ran for 400 performances, it was visited by the King and Queen, and Lord Charnwood, Lincoln's biographer, set on the play the seal of his approval. Its success brought Drinkwater fame; the production in America, which was even more successful, added fortune; but his gain was Barry Jackson's loss, for the successful author naturally gave up his gruelling job as producer and manager at Birmingham.

It is very doubtful whether Barry Jackson or the Birmingham Repertory Theatre made any money out of *Abraham Lincoln*, and Sir Nigel Playfair admits to only a modest profit. The play showed London, however, that the provinces were not merely the home of second-rate touring companies, but that they contained theatres in which something of original imaginative value was being fostered. Following the great artistic success of *Abraham Lincoln*, Barry Jackson continued the work in Birmingham, producing new plays, encouraging young dramatists, and generally trying to build up a playhouse in what was always regarded by managers as one of the worst theatre towns in England. This important side of the work has been dealt with in Bache Matthews's *History of the Birmingham Repertory Theatre*, and it will be referred to in this volume only so far as it is linked up with the enterprises in London.

14

It was not until the autumn of 1922 that Barry Jackson brought his second production to London, and again it was more or less at the invitation of Nigel Playfair. The previous August Playfair had taken over the Euston Palace of Varieties, opposite King's Cross Station, and, as a compliment to Arnold Bennett, called it the Regent, which was, of course, the name of the theatre built by the " card." It was opened with Mr. Bennett's *Body and Soul*, but the play only ran for three weeks. Again Barry Jackson came to the rescue and took a tenancy of the theatre, starting his career as a London manager with *The Immortal Hour*, the work of a composer who was little known to the general public. Rutland Boughton had been a teacher of singing under Granville Bantock at the Midland Institute, Birmingham ; in addition he was a provocative contributor to the musical journals. His interest in the Arthurian legends drew him to Glastonbury, which had become the centre of visionary ideas, and in 1914 he founded the Glastonbury School of Music-Drama. About that time he composed *The Immortal Hour*, which is founded upon Fiona Macleod's short play on the Celtic legend of Etain, the fairy princess who, wandering through mortal woods in search of " something she knows not what," weds Eochaidh, the high King of Ireland. He is able to hold her for a year, and then she is wooed back to her own people by Midir, the immortal lover. It was a case of sheer inspiration, for Rutland Boughton's music expressed not only the quality of the Celtic story, but something of the strange elusiveness of William Sharp, the literary critic, who succeeded in hiding his dual personality, the poet Fiona Macleod, so cleverly from the world. Barry Jackson was introduced to *The Immortal Hour* by Appleby Matthews, who travelled from Birmingham every day to conduct the opera during its run at the Regent. He changed into evening clothes on the train, and managed to arrive at the theatre just as the lights went down for the overture.

Barry Jackson defied a theatrical superstition by fixing a Friday for his first night. That this particular Friday happened to be the 13th of the month

15

was an additional challenge to the gods of chance. For, however sound the judgment, however ripe the experience, and however propitious the time and place, chance enters extraordinarily into theatrical production. Whether or not this Friday was a lucky day for Barry Jackson, who lost altogether £8,000 on *The Immortal Hour*, it was certainly a fortunate one for London, for the season at the Regent was the beginning of perhaps the most interesting management since the war. It may come as a surprise to those who paid many visits to *The Immortal Hour* that Rutland Boughton's opera was anything but successful for several months after the opening night. Indeed, theatre-goers did not go to the Regent in any great numbers until the "last weeks" were announced. It was withdrawn after 216 performances, owing to the fact that Nigel Playfair had to have possession of the theatre for *The Insect Play*. In the last three weeks it became a cult; its admirers, devotees. Princess Marie Louise, who had seen the piece twenty times, was present with the Princess Helena Victoria on that memorable last night when Barry Jackson was presented with an album containing the signatures of over 200 enthusiasts in the world of art and literature. It was an auspicious beginning to a venture that might have fizzled out in a fortnight if the promoter's wealth had not been commensurate with his faith and ideals.

"What shall I do next? I don't know," Barry Jackson said to the audience. "But we are thinking of bringing a Devonshire comedy to London." Then probably for the only time during his career Barry Jackson was booed. Groans came from the audience; "Bring back *The Immortal Hour*," they shouted. It was revived at the Regent on November 14 of the same year and again on January 28, 1924; in January 1926 at the Kingsway; and for a limited run at the Queen's Theatre in January and February 1932.

It is probably not an exaggeration to say that *The Immortal Hour* created a world record in length of run for a serious work in pure opera form; and its success was an indication of the change in the public taste. Playgoers were tired of the inanities that passed for plays during the war period, and it

16

Costume Design for Midir
in
"The Immortal Hour"

will be recalled that the robust and tuneful *Beggar's Opera* was flourishing at the other end of the town. While it is true that Rutland Boughton's music-drama succeeded on its own merit, it is equally true that it was given every chance. Paul Shelving, whose scenery and costumes contributed a great deal to the romantic atmosphere of the opera, had been with the Birmingham Repertory Theatre since 1919, A. E. Filmer (who was then producer) securing his release from the Army, and the work of one of the finest theatre artists of our day was seen in London for the first time. Barry Jackson produced the opera with imagination and extreme care; but perhaps Gwen Ffrangcon-Davies's performance more than anything else was responsible for the wave of enthusiasm that swept across London after the luke-warm opening.

Miss Ffrangcon-Davies, who is the daughter of the famous singer, had sung the part at Glastonbury, and it was at the recommendation of the composer that she was invited to join the Birmingham Repertory Company when the opera was produced. After the run of *The Immortal Hour* she was made a permanent member of the dramatic company, creating Eve in *Back to Methuselah*, and afterwards playing Juliet in the revival of *Romeo and Juliet*—two parts that she later played in London. Miss Ffrangcon-Davies was hailed as a great discovery; she was that rare combination, a singer who could act. She brought to the part of Etain the strange, elusive, elfin quality that meant the difference between success and failure. It is difficult to imagine *The Immortal Hour* without her. Harold Knight painted her as Etain, and the picture now hangs in the Cardiff Art Gallery.

The extraordinary appeal of Mr. Boughton's opera could be illustrated by dozens of stories, but perhaps the most significant tribute was to be found in the manager's lost-property office during one of the runs. Many strange things are found under the seats of most theatres, but the record during *The Immortal Hour* must be unique. There were bags of household goods, packets of sandwiches and, of course, coats, furs, gloves, umbrellas, and opera glasses in profusion. Several women went out leaving their hats behind;

17

and one man left the theatre on a bitterly wet night without his overcoat, hat, and umbrella. On one occasion a box containing twelve sitting eggs was discovered under a seat at the Regent, and other things found by the cleaners were several parcels of underclothing and a packet of ants' eggs ! It shows that the people were so transported into the world of faery that they forgot everything. The illusion lasted until after they left the theatre. During the first run at the Regent it is a fact that two regular members of the audience earned the money to pay for their seats by entertaining the pit queues before the doors opened.

During the first run of *The Immortal Hour* a series of twenty-four matinée performances was given in the Christmas holidays of Barry Jackson's children's entertainment *The Christmas Party*, which had been successfully played at Birmingham. It was a real attempt to provide a gay seasonable attraction. The two youngsters, Chris and Vangy, are down with measles and pretend to give a party in which Santa Claus, Cinderella, Noah, the Three Blind Mice, Old King Cole, with several other nursery heroes, play games, romp, and enjoy such fun as never was. A number of well-known actors were first introduced to London audiences in this jolly entertainment, for the cast included Scott Sunderland as a dustman and also the clown in the old-time Harlequinade, Margaret Chatwin as the Fine Lady from Banbury Cross, Ivor Barnard who doubled Anthony Rowley with Pantaloon, and Hedley Briggs, the dancer, as Colonel MacMashit. The press was practically unanimous in its praise. *The Times* said: " Mr. Barry Jackson has not only tried to construct an entertainment that will appeal to children. He has become a child again himself, and the play should be as popular with the young as any children's play that has been seen in London." The paper added that it was London's loss that *The Christmas Party* had not been seen before. After such eulogistic notices it is a wonder that this entertainment has not been staged again with Lester Pinchard's music and Guy Kortright's delightful costumes.

18

The dramatic critics were quick to recognise the outstanding importance of Barry Jackson's entry into the London theatre, and in June 1923 he was the chief guest at their annual dinner. Bernard Shaw, who had also been invited, replied laconically on a post card : " Boys, I am one with you." Barry Jackson was scarcely complimentary to the metropolis on that occasion, although he confessed that the reception given to *The Immortal Hour* had shaken his belief that London was a place without a soul. He added that he did not intend to stay, as he was afraid of being tarnished by the evil of long runs. Luckily he did stay, possibly because he had heard of the plot that was hatched in the bar of the Regent one evening by Sir E. Denison Ross and another conspirator to sandbag him and keep him here ! The public was clamouring to hear *The Immortal Hour* again, and in November his company was back at the Regent for five weeks' run of Rutland Boughton's opera, which was to be followed at Christmas by the same composer's *Bethlehem*, originally produced at Glastonbury on December 28, 1915. At the time Barry Jackson contemplated a revival of *Cosi fan Tutte*—which had been done some time before in Birmingham—as the first of a series of Mozart operas, an idea that was afterwards carried out by W. Johnstone-Douglas during Barry Jackson's long tenancy of the Court Theatre.

In *The Immortal Hour* Rutland Boughton found inspiration in the Celtic legends; for *Bethlehem* he went to the beginnings of English drama. The Coventry play of the Nativity was freely adapted, and the music drama was divided into six parts, depicting the story from the Annunciation to the departure for Egypt. A good deal of the music was an arrangement of traditional melodies and carols, and Rutland Boughton conducted throughout the comparatively short run. Many of the critics objected to the inclusion of the oriental ballet in Herod's court, but on the whole *Bethlehem* was well received by the press and the distinguished first-night audience. The public did not, however, flock to the theatre, except to the cheaper seats, thus confirming, by the way, the plea that Barry Jackson had been making for a

19

theatre in which the pit should extend to the footlights. Gwen Ffrangcon-Davies's performance as the Rossetti-like Virgin and her " still, cool " acting impressed those people who had admired her as Etain. The company included Frank Titterton as Herod, W. Johnstone-Douglas as Joseph, and Colin Ashdown as Gabriel. It was produced by Barry Jackson under some difficulties, for during the early rehearsals he was taken ill with influenza, and directed the piece by signals from the room he had taken in an hotel near the theatre. From time to time messages were sent across to him, and he replied by a series of signals from the window.

Possibly the request to the audience " not to applaud " *Bethlehem* militated against its box-office success, for it undoubtedly frightened away holiday-makers who were in search of Christmas entertainment. It was against the spirit of the dedication of the score : " To my children and to all children," for children—of all ages—want to clap their hands when they enjoy a thing. Another thing that may have had something to do with the failure was the removal of the curtain. It always spoils the illusion to do away with a definite beginning and a real ending. The rise of the curtain rivets the attention; it has an important psychological effect on the audience. *Bethlehem* was withdrawn after forty-five performances on Saturday, January 24, 1924, and once more *The Immortal Hour* was put into the bill at the Regent.

The third revival ran until May 17, and five days later *Romeo and Juliet* was staged at the Regent with John Gielgud and Gwen Ffrangcon-Davies as the lovers. It was Barry Jackson's first Shakespearean production in London and his only one to be presented in costume—the " modern dress " renderings of *Hamlet*, *Macbeth*, and *The Taming of the Shrew*, which are an important part of modern theatrical history, will be dealt with in a later chapter. It was the time of the opening of the Wembley Exhibition, and colonial visitors were supposed to be asking to see Shakespeare. Charles B. Cochran had taken the rebuke to heart, and was arranging for the Old Vic

Company to go to the old Oxford for a season; in addition, the New Shakespeare Company was shortly to begin a series of productions at the King's, Hammersmith.

None of these was successful, and although *Romeo and Juliet* was kept going for two months, it cannot be said that the play drew the town. But the production helped to enhance several reputations, and it gave John Gielgud, who was to achieve great things later on in Shakespeare, his first big chance in London. He was just over twenty, had already been seen in two or three parts, and had actually played Romeo for a single performance on a Sunday evening. His movements were a trifle awkward in those days, but he spoke the verse beautifully. And he suggested the impetuosity of youth, just as Gwen Ffrangcon-Davies brought to Juliet all the exquisite loveliness of "the child's unstained ideal of love"—to quote *The Times* critic. Except for one or two papers there was a chorus of praise for her performance. J. T. Grein objected that she was not the passionate young Italian girl of fourteen, but to most people this Juliet was the realisation of a dream. She was like a rose first seen in the bud that unfolds itself at the call of the sun and comes to its full glory in the grief of Romeo's banishment. The *Morning Post* described her as "an ideal Juliet, ethereally beautiful, as delicate as porcelain, soft-voiced, and soft-eyed. Tender, serious youth is the keynote of her performance. . . ." The *Evening Standard* had a column leading article of praise, and two papers talked of Juliet being at last " made concrete on the stage," which was perhaps not the happiest way of putting it. The writers meant well, however. Hubert Griffith, who was later to become chief champion of the " modern dress " productions—even to the extent of writing a little book on the subject— declared that the new Juliet was a sophisticated, querulous child, who made the mistake of acting the part. Shakespeare's heroines, he declared, need only be heard; it did not even matter if they were seen. All that was wanted was a darkened stage and a sufficient sense of rhythm to understand the metre of a hymn. Shakespeare, in writing the parts, allowed for the fact that they

21

were to be played by boys. Why Mr. Griffith assumed that the boys could not act cannot be said.

Soon after the opening John Gielgud was forced to leave the cast through illness. His place was taken for a fortnight by Ion Swinley, then at the Vic, who was generously released by Lilian Baylis to step into the breach at short notice, and afterwards by another fine Shakespearean actor, Ernest Milton. Barry Jackson was fortunate in getting their services, but changes such as these are always disconcerting to the public.

A fairly full version of the play was used, and there was only one interval in a performance that lasted well over three hours. H. K. Ayliff was the producer, and Paul Shelving, in his simple, dignified settings, realised that Shakespeare's own verse decorations did not call for much help from the scene designer.

CHAPTER III

TAKING OVER THE COURT—" BACK TO METHUSELAH "—THE AUTHOR'S
MUSICAL ANNOTATION

SEVERAL months before he gave up the tenancy of the Regent, Barry Jackson had taken over the Court in Sloane Square. It was a little theatre with an eventful history. Twenty years before there had been the celebrated Vedrenne-Barker season which had lasted nearly three years. During that period some of the greatest plays of modern times were produced, and it was then that Bernard Shaw was presented to the general public as a dramatist. It is of interest to record that of the 988 performances given during the Vedrenne-Barker season 701 were of Shaw's plays, of which eleven were staged, several of them for the first time. *Heartbreak House* also had its original production at the Court in 1921.

To open therefore on February 18, 1924, with four complete cycles of *Back to Methuselah* was as appropriate as it was adventurous. This vast " metabiological pentateuch "—possibly the longest play written outside China since the three parts of *Henry VI*—had been published in 1922, and first produced in this country at the Birmingham Repertory Theatre in the autumn of 1923.

When Barry Jackson originally asked permission to put on the play, G. B. S. had replied :

" Mr. Jackson, are your wife and children provided for ? "

Back to Methuselah had already been seen in America, for the Theatre Guild of New York had asked Shaw for a contract before the play was published. He sent one of his characteristic replies :

23

"A contract is unnecessary. It isn't likely that any other lunatics will want to produce it."

When the Guild started rehearsals G. B. S. wrote a long letter, in which he said they must make up their minds to give separate performances, and suggested that tickets should be sold in batches, all five tickets on one sheet with perforated card divisions.

"Later on we can see about giving separate performances of the sections; but for the first ten performances (say) it must be impossible to take less than the whole dose."

But this advice was not followed. The drama was divided into three sections, and Parts 1 and 2 were played the first week, Parts 3 and 4 in the second, and Part 5 in the third week finished the cycle.

When the preliminary negotiations were being made for the production at Birmingham, Mr. Shaw wrote the following letter to Cyril Phillips, who was in charge of the arrangements:

"I am strongly of opinion that tickets for the first two *Methuselah* sets should be sold in blocks only, possibly at special prices. If the prices are special they could be arranged so that it would not matter whether the ticket for the first matinée were called complimentary or not. If the prices were normal, the complimentary matinée would be only in the nature of a discount. I do not foresee any objection either way; but I think we should refuse to sell single tickets for the first set or two, and even for the first three or four if the sets for the first two went off very well.

"As to London, I wish I could believe that there is the slightest likelihood of your finding yourself up against any serious competitor there. Mr. Mac-dermott of the Everyman Theatre talks of taking the Little Theatre and trying his fortune there. If he does that, he may covet *Methuselah*; but if Mr. Barry Jackson is keen on losing some more money in the Regent Theatre, I should

24

be very favourably disposed; in fact, if somebody is to be ruined, I had rather it were B. J. than anyone else.

"G. Bernard Shaw."

The method of selling seats for the whole cycle and devoting five consecutive evenings to the play was certainly the better one, for it preserved a sense of continuity. It was justified by the results, for the theatre was crowded for the first week, and did exceedingly well during the month's run. Before the rehearsals began at the Repertory Theatre Barry Jackson and H. K. Ayliff called on Mr. Shaw in London to discuss the cast and the production, and they were surprised to find that he kept a card-index of actors and actresses which he consulted from time to time. It was his original intention to attend all the rehearsals in Birmingham, but during a holiday in Ireland he slipped on some rocks and broke two ribs which kept him away from the theatre until the dress rehearsals. There were several letters from him, and in one he said : " Note that the people in *Methuselah* are not Coué-ists willing to live 300 years. The people who begin it are a parson and a housemaid who are both taken entirely by surprise by their longevity. The people who believe in it do not survive." In another, he replies very amusingly to the suggestion that, as the first part of *Methuselah* was rather short for an evening's entertainment, it should be preceded by a lecture from the author or some other literary celebrity :

" Dear Mr. Phillips,
    " Remember the negro who said, ' If preachee, preachee; if floggee, floggee; but no preachee floggee too.' If you want to open the Methuselah proceedings by a public meeting, take the Town Hall, and get Chesterton if you can; but don't mix up dramatic entertainment in the theatre with politics. If the programme is too short, put on an opera as a curtain raiser; but if there are to be speeches and literary stars, then I think the actors, whose show it properly is, will have a grievance; and I will beat a precipitate retreat. I never take an author's call nowadays. I hold the mixture of play and meeting in

25

special horror; and I speak in theatres (as on the R.U.R. occasion) only when there is no performance on.

" What became of Mr. Jackson's notion of making the Adam and Eve show an invitation occasion for purchasers of sets of tickets ?

" Unless Chesterton is quite mad, he will refuse to come on *after* Adam and Eve and Cain. The effect would be ghastly.

" I shall be at this address until about the third week in September, when I shall break away for Birmingham and look in at the rehearsals. I am wiring this change in my plans to Mr. Ayliff. Nothing must be said publicly about my interfering in the production : the whole credit (and responsibility) must go to the Repertory Theatre. I shall not meddle except as far as I can be helpful about odds and ends.

" I am of course open to consultation by letter; but the posts here are slow and precarious.

" I must stay here until my new play is finished.

" Faithfully,

" G. BERNARD SHAW."

He also had some correspondence with Mr. Ayliff, and the chief point of contention between the author and the producer concerned the staging of the Serpent in Part 1. Edith Evans had been chosen to play the part in Birmingham, and Mr. Shaw was firmly of opinion that her face should not be seen by the audience, and drew a picture of his idea of the Serpent for Mr. Ayliff's guidance. After a good deal of discussion it was agreed that the producer should carry out his own plan and if Mr. Shaw disapproved at the dress rehearsal the scene was to be altered. When he arrived at the theatre he was intensely interested in Edith Evans's make-up and the scene was passed without question. Mr. Ayliff, who has produced so many of Mr. Shaw's plays, has said that the directions given in the printed versions are absolutely right and can rarely be improved upon—even by the author himself.

26

It was during this visit to Birmingham, by the way, that G. B. S. was lost for several hours. When he arrived he told Barry Jackson that he was anxious to see the topical film of a prize-fight that he heard was being shown. Enquiries were made at the chief cinemas, but none of them was exhibiting the picture. Mr. Shaw discovered that it was to be seen at some outlying cinema and, without saying a word to anyone, found the place, paid his shilling, and saw the film. He returned to find that search parties were being formed to look for him !

There was an amusing incident at the end of the first cycle at Birmingham which has not been recorded before. When the curtain was finally rung down the author stood on the stage with the company that included Edith Evans, Cedric Hardwicke, and the other brilliant players who had sustained the long parts. Before anyone had a chance to say a word a young super who was making her first appearance on the stage stepped forward, shook Mr. Shaw by the hand and said, " Allow me to congratulate you on the success of your play." " Everybody "—to use Barry Jackson's words—" was flabbergasted." There is a sequel to the story. The young woman, who had little to recommend her as an actress except some startling good looks, was a few years later a member of the chorus of Ziegfield's Follies.

The play was given at the Court with practically the same cast as at Birmingham, and G. B. S. attended all the rehearsals. It has been recorded by Bache Matthews that the members of the company at the Repertory Theatre were terrified by the thought of the author's arrival, but when he came they found him extraordinarily kind and appreciative. It is doubtful if any dramatist is as helpful at rehearsals as G. B. S.; for one thing, he never interrupts during the playing of a scene. Usually he sits in the front row of the dress-circle with a big note-book. At the end of a section he goes down to the stage and immediately puts the actors at their ease by giving quiet individual advice, carefully crossing through each note after it has been disposed of. He is a wonderful actor himself, and can show the players how the parts should be

27

acted. Once at a rehearsal of *Major Barbara*, he took over the part of Adolphus Cusins at the end of the Salvation Army scene, giving an imitation of the professor of Greek playing the trombone, and on another occasion, during a walk along a country road G. B. S. described to the writer the in-anities of a film he had just seen by imitating some of the actors. He goes to endless trouble to get a character played according to his conception, and it is well known that he insists on every syllable being given its proper value. It would not be a misstatement to say that he orchestrates the parts for the actors, and in one instance he actually annotated a copy of the play in musical terms. This was for Scott Sunderland who appeared as Cain in Act 2 of the first part of *Back to Methuselah*, and as the Elderly Gentleman in Part 4.

G. B. S. had discovered that Mr. Sunderland shared his passion for music, and these are some of the instructions written in Mr. Shaw's fine, upright, sensitive handwriting in that actor's copy of the play.

It will be remembered that Act 2 of Part 1 is set in an oasis in Mesopotamia, with Eve sitting on a stool spinning, and Adam digging in the garden. Cain's voice is heard as the curtain rises, and Mr. Shaw has written this introductory note :

" Cain should open this scene in a quite modern vein, with the high-pitch and haw-haw of a stage cavalry officer, and with conceited superiority and self-satisfaction. He is not a savage. By contrast with Adam he is a highly civilized gentleman. He does not scowl; his swagger is a gay swagger. He patronises his parents."

The actor is told to pitch his first long speech—" Whose fault was it that I killed Abel . . ."—" say, in, C Major." " He is to be happy and con-descending." When he gets down to the line, " I envied his happiness, his freedom . . ." he is told to " drop without modulation to A flat, and abandon all affectation. He is now *talking about himself*, and much more serious than when he was talking about Abel."

28

Mr. Shaw's next comment is against Cain's protest, " I do not want to kill women. I do not want to kill my mother. . . ." The actor is to be " reasonable for the first two sentences : then a little savage," and in the following speech he is to " begin at a low pitch and drag the time a little ; then take the whole speech as a *crescendo—p.* to *ff.*" Against the words "fighting, fighting, killing, killing !" there is a note : " *martellato,*" and after " burning, overwhelming life," Mr. Shaw has written " *meno mosso.*"

One of the most interesting clues to the character of Cain is in the following note :

" Always making a difference between his tone to his mother, which is affectionate, and to his father, which is ruthlessly contemptuous."

Mr. Shaw has written this against the line : " Mother ; the making of men is your right, your risk, your glory, your triumph. . . ."

When Cain talks about " hero and superman " he is " again the cavalry officer," and later when he replies to Adam's expostulation about the " voice of Death "—" it whispers to me that death is not really death : that it is the gate of another life "—he is told to " strike a new note. The *steigerung* is now poetic, dreamy, visionary, the impetus got by intensity rather than speed."

With the line, " I revolt against the clay," he is to reach " his top note ; it is the climax—and indeed the end—of this part. His style in this speech is large and grand and harmonious, in longer bars, a little restrained in speed, but otherwise all out."

I have quoted a few of the more important notes—leaving out most of the technical musical terms that are scattered through the part—in order to give a practical illustration of Mr. Shaw's thoroughness. It is, of course, unusual for him to go to the length of a musical annotation—in this case it was a compliment to Mr. Sunderland's love of Mozart—but he often writes one of his famous post cards to tell an actor something he has forgotten to mention at a rehearsal.

One thing that Mr. Shaw will not have is slovenliness of diction. His own voice is extremely pleasant and his diction perfect. No clipping of the ends of words, or running them together is tolerated by the author of some of the best stage speeches in the language.

It is extraordinary how sadly misinformed some of the paragraph writers are about G. B. S. On the day of the production of *Back to Methuselah* a journalist wondered whether the author would attend the London *première* of his play-cycle, and went on to say that Mr. Shaw found *Heartbreak House* too long for him. Everyone who knows anything at all about him knows that G. B. S. prefers his own plays to anybody else's. Although he had sat right through *Methuselah* twice at Birmingham and again at the London rehearsals, he was the most eager member of the audience at that memorable first week at the Court. It was indeed a unique occasion; a play that ran for five consecutive nights. Since that date, however, the same sort of thing has happened at Malvern, where for a week the same people have sat next to each other night after night at the theatre.

To say that *Back to Methuselah* was well received by the critics would be to make a gross misstatement; but it is interesting to note that E. A. Baughan, who had seen the whole cycle both at Birmingham and in London, was full of praise for " a noble achievement of which the British stage may be proud." It is obviously a play that improves on better acquaintance; at the same time there was no excuse for the levity with which it was treated by some of the writers who were seeing it for the first time. One of them expressed his feelings in a jingle, the first verse of which read :

> " Our G. B. S. so jabbered and jawed,
> As the air with his mental arms he sawed,
> That hundreds present were drinkward ' drawed '—
> Crying, " Back, Back to Bar-thuselah."

30

To at least half of the critics the five nights were a huge joke. Notices took the form of bulletins from the Sloane Square Front—"' The worst is now over,' writes our correspondent," was one example. " Is there nobody to stop G. B. S. ?" was a sub-headline to an article that ended : " Will relief never come ?" A great deal of nonsense was written about the play being a " test of endurance " whereas—as Hubert Griffith pointed out in *The Observer*—"first-nighters have often been asked to sit out five successive nights of new plays, often of the ghastliest quality, *Methuselah* at any rate is administered in small homœopathic doses." The general feeling was that Parts 1 and 5 were finely impressive pieces of work, worthy of Shaw's genius, which reached the high-water mark of achievement in Lilith's valedictory speech. " As noble a piece of prose as Mr. Shaw has ever written," was Ivor Brown's verdict in a long critical article in *The Saturday Review*. Beverley Baxter, who was then writing for the *Sunday Express*, said that " to have written those lines alone would place the author among the immortals of English letters." Mr. Baxter added that he was certain that *Back to Methuselah* would be performed many decades hence, but as a long one-night play, with Parts 2, 3, and 4 omitted. It is of interest to mention here that in the New York production it was Part 2, about which Mr. Shaw had expressed a doubt for American audiences, that was the most popular. In Berlin it created such a *furore* that the manager broke his contract and ran it night after night, abandoning the rest of the pentateuch.

At the end of the first week at Birmingham G. B. S. marked the occasion as exceptional by breaking his rule against taking authors' calls and making a speech from the stage, and when the curtain was down he did a step dance for the benefit of the company.

After the opening night in London Barry Jackson announced that the author would speak at the end of the cycle ; but G. B. S. held to his rule as absolute for London. Perhaps he had heard that some of the younger and brighter critics had hatched a plot to appear in their seats on the Friday as " Methuselahs " in wigs and beards by Clarkson, and were only dissuaded from doing so at the last minute. Instead of a speech from the stage he gave an interview to the press the following week, in which he is reported to have said :

" It is unthinkable that a man of my age would devote two whole years to a petty joke. I am only a leg puller in so far as I pull crooked legs straight.

" The public are all mental cripples, and if they question the reasons that prompted me to write *Back to Methuselah* it only affords a striking illustration of my opinion expressed in that play that the English race has never become fully adult."

He said he did not see why the mere fact that the play took five nights for its performance should be regarded as surprising.

" Was not Wagner's *Ring* composed for four nights ? " he asked. " If I felt like it," he went on to say, " I would write a play that would take a month to perform. Why shouldn't I ? The only objection is the purely technical one of the difficulty of rehearsing so many plays simultaneously and paying for the large cast necessary.

" When I wrote my first play thirty-two years ago," he said indignantly, " the critics and the whole town were in an uproar for a fortnight. Now people who see it cannot understand what all the fuss was about. It will be the same with *Methuselah*.

" I wrote it because I meant it all. Why does Sargent paint pictures ? Why did Shakespeare write plays ? I have the specific talent for being a dramatist, and I choose to use the medium of the drama to say what I think.

" Many years ago perhaps there was some justification for calling some of my work ridiculous. But now, after I have written for over thirty years, and my plays have been produced in all parts of the world, it is absurd to treat me as though I were a gutter-snipe. Yet that is now the accepted way of treating me. Either that or saying that I am growing old and dull.

" Of course it is flattering to find columns written about the smallest

32

Costume Design for Amanda
in
" A Trip to Scarborough "

details and changes in the food that I eat and the clothes I wear, the fact that I am six-foot tall, treating me, in fact, as though I am the one exception to the whole human race. None the less, it is an infernal nuisance."

It was, of course, only a section of the Press against which Mr. Shaw hurled his invective, and in this connection it is interesting to read what he has to say in the preface about dramatic criticism.

" The worst convention of the criticism of the theatre current at that time," he wrote, referring to the opening of the present century, " was that intellectual seriousness is out of place on the stage; that the theatre is a place of shallow amusement; that people go there to be soothed after the enormous intellectual strain of a day in the city; in short, that a playwright is a person whose business it is to make unwholesome confectionery out of cheap emotions."

The fact that the wretched little verse quoted on page 30 could appear in a reputable paper is a proof that there was certainly justification for Mr. Shaw's objection to being treated like a " gutter-snipe." The more dignified journals had their own complaints. Mr. Walkley objected to the inclusion of Lubin and Joyce Burge in Part 2, which he described as a " breach of good manners"; he was also upset by Eileen Beldon's pronunciation of the word " isolate " in the fourth part. This was followed by Edward Marsh's letter to *The Times*:

" Many of your readers will have welcomed the trouncing given by your Dramatic Critic this morning to Mr. Bernard Shaw for the personal allusions which disfigure the second part of *Back to Methuselah*. The most painful of these to Mr. Shaw's admirers was the passage in which (without any disguise of the persons aimed at) he pours his especial scorn on the ' Politician' who actually allowed his son to get killed in the war. At this point Mr. Shaw seems to part company not only with decency but with sense; for somebody must be killed in a war, and surely the statesman who allows his own child

33

to sacrifice himself is more, and not less, admirable than one who saves his family at the expense of others."

Mr. Shaw replied to the critic and to his friend Mr. Marsh in a letter to *The Times.*

" I am very reluctant to make any comment on the expressions of irritation which my play at the Court Theatre must inevitably provoke from the short-lived, but Mr. Edward Marsh, whose sensibilities I have every personal reason for respecting, must not accuse me of pouring scorn on the politician who actually allowed his son to be killed in the war. In what sense did any man ' allow ' his son to be killed in the war ? Would any man have allowed such a thing if he could have prevented it ? Many men, who were more or less responsible for the war, had that responsibility brought home to them by the loss of a well-beloved son; but they will hardly, I think, regard that as a fact to be suppressed as shameful, or deny the son his right to his record and his share in the moral of the greatest tragedy of his time. Does Mr. Marsh really believe that his delicacy is greater and more consoling than mine when he dismisses the son with the remark that ' somebody must be killed in a war,' and treats his fate as a mere personal episode in which a father ' allows his own child to sacrifice himself '; and is it to be contrasted with ' one who saves his family at the expense of others ' ? In the framework of my play such phrases would be heartless nonsense: the case is bigger and deeper than that.

" As to ' pouring scorn ' on anyone, what I have done is to exhibit our Parliamentary politics in contrast with politics SUB SPECIE ÆTERNITATIS. If under this test they shrink to a ridiculous smallness and reveal a disastrous inadequacy, that is not a reason why the exposure should be spared: it is a more urgent reason for submitting them to it ruthlessly. And as the dramatic method requires that the politics should be expounded by politicians, and the test can be valid only if the politicians are recognizably true to historic fact, the politicians to some extent must share the fate of the politics. This inevitable effect may scandalize the critics who, being innocent of political life, imagine that statesmen approach elections with their minds wholly pre-occupied with abstract principles, oblivious to the existence of such persons as voters, and most undemocratically indifferent to their likes and dislikes. Such critics imagine that in representing two ex-premiers, on the eve of a General Election, as keenly alive to such considerations, and only too bitterly aware of our electoral ignorance, folly, and gullibility, I am representing them as un-principled scoundrels; but I can hardly be expected to defer to a judgment so ludicrously uninstructed. My play, as far as it goes outside the public history of public men, contains not a word against the private honor of any living person; and if I do not share the delicacy as to equally public and politically active women which restrained Silas Wegg from going into details concerning the Decline and Fall of the Roman Empire, I can only say that my blue pencil is at the service of any lady who can find a single reference to herself which is not within the privilege of the friendliest good humor.

"I have been accused in your columns of 'Shouting scandal from the housetops.' Is it scandal to say of one statesman that he is happily married? or of another, who has an almost embarrassingly clever and famous wife, and two daughters whose achievements in politics and literature threaten to eclipse his own, that he is in this fortunate condition? Surely my apology is due to these ladies for having given them minor and even mute parts in a drama in which they actually played much more important ones, and not to your critic, who grudges them any mention at all. It is true that in stage fiction many marriages are scandalous, and most of them triangular. The critic's mind becomes at last like the dyer's hand: the wedding-ring suggests nothing to him but the Divorce Court. But my plays are not theatrical plays in that sense; and I hope an honest woman may be mentioned in them without a stain on her character.

"Finally, as Miss Eileen Beldon has been accused by your critic of mis-pronouncing the word 'isolate' (perhaps he rhymes it, as many do, to 'why

35

so late '), may I ask him how he pronounces it himself ?   I once asked Thomas Hardy how he pronounced The Dynasts. He replied that he called it The Dinnasts, but that so many people know no better than to call it the Die-nasts that he was getting shy of it, and preferred not to mention it at all. I appeal to your critic not to make Miss Beldon shy, and, after consulting the pronouncing dictionaries, to send her a suitable apology."

It must be remembered it was *Back to Methuselah* that brought the Birmingham Repertory Company to town, although several members had been seen in the productions at the Regent.   Cedric Hardwicke had taken one or two small parts before the war, but he made what was practically his first appearance in London at the Court as Haslam, the curate in Part 2, and the He-Ancient in the final section.   Gwen Ffrangcon-Davies had by then established her reputation in *The Immortal Hour* and *Romeo and Juliet*, and it was enhanced by the beauty of her Eve and the transparent innocency of her acting in the final scene.   Other performances that stood out memorably were those of Mr. Scott Sunderland, as the Elderly Gentleman, a superb piece of acting of a part that defeated the player in the New York production, Mr. Colin Keith-Johnston as Adam, of Frank Moore, Wallace Evennett, Leo Carroll, and Evelyn Hope, to mention a few of the players more or less at random.   Possibly the crowning experience of the week was the austere loveliness of Margaret Chatwin's rendering of Lilith's speech at the end.

When the first and last parts were revived at the Court for a series of matinées at the end of 1924 Edith Evans was then free to repeat the performance as the Serpent and the She-Ancient, the parts she had taken in the original production at Birmingham.

CHAPTER IV

"THE FARMER'S WIFE"

*B*ACK TO METHUSELAH may be described as the intellectual house-warming for the homelier fare of *The Farmer's Wife*—the Devonshire comedy mentioned in the speech at the end of *The Immortal Hour*—which opened on March 11, and ran for 1,329 performances—the third longest run of a straight play in the history of the English theatre, the record having been beaten only by *Charley's Aunt* and *Our Boys*. Although this was his thirteenth play to be seen in London, it marked the beginning of the Eden Phillpotts era; yet, if *The Farmer's Wife* had not been carefully "nursed" through the first few weeks, when it was played to audiences composed almost entirely of "dead-heads," it would not have lasted a month.

The history of *The Farmer's Wife* provides an instructive commentary on the curious insularity of the London theatre managers. The comedy, first performed at Birmingham in 1916, had been the most persistent success in the company's repertory, yet nobody in London had made any attempt to produce it. It is doubtful if many people outside Birmingham had heard of the play. In Germany every big city is a producing centre, and if a piece succeeds in one theatre it is rapidly staged all over the country. To the London managers the theatre is confined to what is called the West End, the Provinces being the places to which second- and third-rate touring companies are sent.

Eden Phillpotts wrote the play in 1912. He had just added another volume to the series of Dartmoor novels on which he was then engaged, and he determined to make a play out of the abundant material in *Widdecombe Fair*. Of the fifty characters in the book he used twenty, and one of the many themes of that famous story. To use his own words: "It travelled the usual way,

37

handled by many postmen, to such managements as were disposed to read it, but it returned again and again with increasing depression from those journeys, until, so weary did the manuscript become, that it had to be re-typed and polished up before taking the road again."

At one stage of its career the manuscript reached Edmund Gwenn, who wanted it for himself and Hilda Trevelyan, then at the Vaudeville, but Messrs. Gatti, the owners of the theatre, did not like the thought of peasants in the Strand, and it went back to the author. After it had been discarded for some time Eden Phillpotts handed the manuscript to A. E. Drinkwater—John Drinkwater's father—who gave it to Barry Jackson. The first production took place at the Repertory Theatre on November 11, 1916, and it had been revived five times before the London presentation.

A. E. Drinkwater died in January 1923, and it was a tragedy that he never lived to produce *The Farmer's Wife* in London and see the success of the comedy upon which he had worked so hard. The play had to be cut, and to some extent it had been reconstructed by A. E. Drinkwater; H. K. Ayliff also made further alterations for the Court. The production was in the tradition, however, and he had the advantage of having in the company Margaret Chatwin, Isabel Thornton, and Maud Gill, who were members of the original cast, and many of the actors who had appeared in the subsequent revivals. Some of them had just been seen in *Back to Methuselah*. So little was known about *The Farmer's Wife* before it opened that, despite the announcement that the play was a comedy, several writers in the press anticipated a sombre evening. "There is something in the air of Dartmoor that seems to make the most humorous writer dull," was one cheerful paragraph that immediately preceded the production. Besides, the play was being put on by Barry Jackson, the man who staged *The Immortal Hour*, *Romeo and Juliet*, and *Back to Methuselah*, works which, however excellent, were none of them particularly hilarious. The fun on the first night, edged as it was by farce, came as a pleasant surprise, and next day the critics were on the whole enthusiastic.

The comedy might be uneven, amateurish, a trifle discursive, a burlesque rather than a picture of life in Devonshire, but it was genuinely funny and enjoyable, and the general effect was pleasant and homely. *The Times* said: " Mr. Phillpotts may not always make us live in the Applegarth Farm, but we greatly enjoyed looking through the window," which seemed to express the general opinion.

The theme of *The Farmer's Wife* is based upon the oldest of stories—that of a man who goes out in search of romance and after many adventures returns to find what he sought in his own kitchen. As a plot it held little in the way of surprise, for the end was foreseen almost as soon as the play opened; but the joy of the piece lay in the racy characterisation and the broad rustic humour that was seasoned with the salt of life. The names of the characters were redolent of the soil: Araminta Dench, Thirza Tapper, Sibley Sweetland, Valiant Dunnybrig, and the immortal Churdles Ash brought with them the tang of Devonshire. The second act introduced to Londoners the now familiar Phillpotts's tea-party, but certainly the best thing in the play was the character of the " battered and crusty henchman, Churdles Ash," one of the most thorough misogynists ever seen on the stage.

A good deal of the credit for the stage success of this part must go to Cedric Hardwicke, who had just before been seen—practically for the first time in London—as another " He-Ancient "—in the last part of *Back to Methuselah*. James Agate in the *Sunday Times* said of the performance that the part " was beautifully played by Cedric Hardwicke. Old Churdles Ash might have come straight out of Borrow, or, again, you could imagine cantankerous Samuel Butler taking him to his heart. . . . There was one moment when, some twenty people being assembled on the stage, one forgot, or almost forgot, about the theatre, and fell to thinking in terms of some native, endeared village. There is tribute here, not only to the player who fused the acting round about him to a sensible whole, but to the producer, whose stage-picture at this point was a masterly piece of composition."

39

Except for an excursion into the glamorous world of musical comedy at Drury Lane Cedric Hardwicke has been in Barry Jackson's company ever since the war. When he played Churdles Ash he was only known in London for his performance in *Back to Methuselah*, and in the seven years since that date he has established himself as one of the leading actors on the English stage. Cedric Hardwicke is a " star," and several of *The Farmer's Wife* company are well known, but they were not when the play was produced at the Court. The production exhibited the value of the repertory training and what can be accomplished in team-work by the members of a company who were used to acting together. Of the individual performances those of Melville Cooper (later to add to his reputation as Trotter in *Journey's End*) as the farmer who " would a-wooing go," Evelyn Hope as the charmingly capable housekeeper, Maud Gill as Thirza Tapper, Margaret Chatwin as the fox-hunting widow, Scott Sunderland and Colin Keith-Johnston as the two young lovers, and Phyllis Shand and Eileen Beldon as the Sweetland girls, still stand out vividly in the memory. It is interesting to note that the very small part of the Hon. Mrs. Tudor was taken by Frances Doble, who had just before been seen in *Methuselah*, and that Sibley Sweetland's song, " Blue Eyes," was composed by that fine actor, Lawrence Hanray, who does not seem to have since exercised his gifts in this direction.

During the first three or four months *The Farmer's Wife* was run at a loss. The expenses were low and the deficit therefore not very big; and Barry Jackson was encouraged to keep it running because the takings increased a little each week. What eventually turned the tide was a campaign of clever poster advertising, and tube stations and hoardings were liberally plastered with slogans printed in black block letters on a yellow surface:

" THE FARMER'S WIFE
IS THE LAUGH OF YOUR LIFE "

was the first, and for this Cedric Hardwicke was responsible. A good many originated from Raymond Pierpont, who was business manager at the Court, and the fever spread to Barry Jackson himself who thought of:

"HAVE YOU BEEN TO
THIRZA TAPPER'S TEA-PARTY?"

When the hundredth performance was reached early in June it became fairly evident that *The Farmer's Wife* would stay at the Court, and a month later—during a heat-wave—the "house-full" boards were out. At the end of the first year Cedric Hardwicke gave up the part of Churdles Ash in order that he might appear in *Cæsar and Cleopatra*, and his place was taken by that excellent character actor, Charles Groves. On November 9, 1925, the King and Queen visited the play at the Court Theatre, and laughed heartily throughout the evening. Perhaps the most astonishing thing in the history of *The Farmer's Wife* is that the play has never been seen by its author, although, at A. E. Drinkwater's wish, he attended some of the original rehearsals in Birmingham. He remained quietly in his home in Devonshire, writing innumerable letters to the staff of the theatre, and taking the opportunity as each century was reached to give a party (at which he was never present) for the company. At the first, Arnold Bennett, an old friend of Phillpotts and a great admirer of *The Farmer's Wife*, was the host, and the courses on the menu-card were prefaced by quotations from the play, mostly remarks by Churdles Ash. When the five-hundred mark was touched Eden Phillpotts wrote the following letter to the company:

"MY DEAR FRIENDS,—

"Heartfelt congratulations on your unique achievement, for no peasant play ever did this before. I drain a foaming beaker of barley water to you, one and all, and beg that you will join me in a glass of something more worthy of the great occasion.

"With affection,
"E. P."

41

It is difficult to say why he has remained one of the few people in England who has not seen *The Farmer's Wife*; one of the reasons given was that his early associations with the theatre had left such painful memories that he had no desire to visit a playhouse again. Even when the touring company was near him in Devonshire Eden Phillpotts could not be induced to pay a visit and see his characters alive on the stage, although he always made a point of inviting the company to lunch at his home.

A tour was sent out by the Birmingham Repertory Theatre early in 1925, and other companies followed. In some cases a town was visited from four to five times. *The Farmer's Wife* was revived for a short season at the Queen's Theatre in 1932.

CHAPTER V

THE KINGSWAY EXPERIMENT—" CÆSAR AND CLEOPATRA "—" THE NEW MORALITY "

IN the spring of 1925, faced with the obstinate success of *The Farmer's Wife* at the Court, and needing a new outlet for the " artistic capital " that was being piled up in Birmingham, Barry Jackson took over the Kingsway for a definite series of productions. By this time he had realised that the Repertory Theatre run on experimental lines could not be made to pay unless it were regarded as a " trying-out " centre for London. A case in point was *Cæsar and Cleopatra*, which had just been staged in Birmingham with lavish scenery and costumes by Paul Shelving. It was obvious that there was a wider public for the revival of Mr. Shaw's " history," which had not been seen since 1913, than could be found in the Midland city.

G. B. S. was on the top of the wave, for even the irreverent people, who had treated *Back to Methuselah* as an elaborate joke, were profoundly impressed by *Saint Joan*, which had been produced at the New Theatre in March 1924 and was then being played at the Regent. The moment was therefore an opportune one for *Cæsar and Cleopatra*. It opened at the Kingsway on April 21, 1925 (a day or two before the 500th performance of *The Farmer's Wife*), with practically the same cast that appeared at Birmingham. The distinguished audience on the first night included Sir Johnston Forbes-Robertson, who had created the part of Cæsar eighteen years before and had made his final salute to the English stage in that play.

Cæsar and Cleopatra, it will be remembered, was one of the early Plays for Puritans, and it was written immediately after the author's marriage in 1898, partly at Hindhead in Surrey, partly in the Isle of Wight, for

Sir Johnston Forbes-Robertson, who was, according to Mr. Shaw, the only actor on the English stage then capable of playing a classical part in the grand manner without losing the charm and lightness of an accomplished comedian. Mrs. Patrick Campbell was to have been the Cleopatra; and accordingly, when the American copyright had to be secured by one of those funny performances—happily abolished by the last Copyright Act—in which the company solemnly walked through the play book in hand before an audience of a single confederate (the public, though nominally welcome to attend, were kept at bay by the announcement " Admission to all parts of the theatre: one guinea," and by the unearthly hour of the performance) the task was undertaken by Mrs. Patrick Campbell's Company in the Theatre Royal, Newcastle-on-Tyne, on March 15, 1899, at 11 a.m. Harley Granville-Barker made his first appearance in a Shaw play as Septimius on this occasion. It is needless to say that the playbill of that performance is now a collector's treasure.

Mrs. Patrick Campbell, however, was not attracted by her part; and nothing further happened with the play until August 1906, when after a delay caused by a vain attempt to secure Gordon Craig as producer, it was performed in Berlin, where the third act threw the audience into a mood of such gaiety that the success of the more tragic fourth act was seriously imperilled.

Three months later Forbes-Robertson made his first appearance in the play at the New Amsterdam Theatre, New York, with Gertrude Elliott as Cleopatra. This was followed by a six months' tour in America, and a three months' tour in the English provinces, after which the play was produced in London in December 1907 at the Savoy Theatre, then under the management of Vedrenne and Barker.

In 1913 Forbes-Robertson bade farewell to the London stage in a series of crowded performances at Drury Lane. At these *Cæsar and Cleopatra* reached its culminating point of success. This was followed by a farewell tour in America, at the conclusion of which the great actor took the huge sphinx which he had had modelled for the first act and the rest of the scenery and burnt them to ashes.

It was assumed by many of the critics that the Prologue written for the Great God Ra, addressed to the " quaint little islanders " who stood " perplexed between an Old England and a New, as Cæsar's Romans stood between an Old Rome and a New," which may be said to epitomise the preface, was written especially for the Kingsway production. It was not then included in the printed version of the play, but in his *Collected Works* Mr. Shaw has given it as an alternative opening. He wrote it for Sir Johnston's farewell performance at Drury Lane. At that time the custom of playing with four intervals and heavy stage " sets " for scenery made it impossible to perform the play at full length. Mr. Shaw therefore agreed to sacrifice the third act—the quay scene in front of the Palace. But as this act was such a success in Berlin, Forbes-Robertson wanted to restore it, so the first scene of Act I was omitted. In 1925 the old intervals had gone out of fashion; and Paul Shelving, as scene designer, was able to provide for a continuous performance with only one interval. The play therefore was presented in its entirety, including the prologue and the third act. It actually played for three and a half hours.

H. K. Ayliff has confessed that he found *Cæsar and Cleopatra* more difficult to produce than *Back to Methuselah*. The Kingsway stage is small and the play called for the vaster reaches of Drury Lane. Paul Shelving's conventional scenery was gay, bright—almost white-hot in its brightness—and perhaps a trifle too shallow. Possibly with the space at his disposal, it was the best way to set the play, but the eye was hungry for the solid proportions of Mr. Rickett's scenery for *Saint Joan*.

It would not be amiss to say that Cæsar is Mr. Shaw in a toga. Cedric Hardwicke, released from the rusticities of Phillpotts, was made up to resemble the bust in the British Museum. He was admirably dignified and incisive both in speech and movement, but he has confessed in his very candid autobiography that he could not shake off Churdles Ash in time for the first performance. He lacked something of wit and freedom; a lighter rendering would have been more in the spirit of Shaw's creation. Certainly he gave a much better performance of Cæsar at the Malvern Festival revival of the play in 1929. But it is a difficult character, whereas Gwen Ffrangcon-Davies, with Cleopatra to play with, had a part that was made for her hands. Half-child, half-woman, with one of the finest " entrances " in modern drama, she was the embodiment of his heroine from the moment that Cleopatra interrupted Cæsar's apostrophe to the Sphinx and asked the " old gentleman " not to run away. She was at once the minx and the woman, her moods alternated from petulant sullenness to amorous sunshine, and there were fine moments of empiric grandeur as when, for instance, she exclaimed, " I will make all my lovers kings."

The best fun in the play is, of course, Britannus, through whom the author indulges in some of his wittiest tilts at the English, and Scott Sunderland (who was allowed by Mr. Shaw to insert a line of his own) was gloriously pompous in the part. Outstanding too was George Hayes as the æsthetic Apollodorus.

The Kingsway had been definitely taken over as an experimental theatre, and the fact that *Cæsar and Cleopatra* was withdrawn on June 27, after only two months' run, was in accordance with Barry Jackson's policy.

The next item in a season which was perhaps the most interesting in London since the Frohman repertory at the Duke of York's was a revival of Harold Chapin's comedy *The New Morality*. This deliciously witty *soufflé* had been staged in 1920 by the Play Actors, a producing society which has now ceased to exist, with Athene Seyler as the jealous wife and J. H. Roberts as her rival's husband, and it was " tried out " again at a matinée performance at the Aldwych the following year, when the casting was not so happy. No really good comedy has ever been so unlucky as *The New Morality*. It is one of the most delightful gems in modern drama, as light as air, almost perfect within its convention, and yet it was only seen for a bare month at the Kingsway. Harold Chapin wrote the play for Marie Tempest, who had appeared in

46

Art and Opportunity in 1912, but she felt that the part did not suit her. It had to wait for production until after the war as far as London was concerned. In the meantime the young author had been killed, for he joined the R.A.M.C. in 1914, and died on the Somme in 1915. Sir James Barrie has referred to him as the " greatest might-have-been " lost to the English stage in the war.

It is difficult to imagine a greater contrast to Mr. Shaw's " history " than this brilliant comedy about a set of modern people on a house-boat. In fact, no greater proof of Barry Jackson's catholicity need be adduced than a recital of the list of the plays produced at the Kingsway : *Cæsar and Cleopatra*, *The New Morality*, *Hamlet* in modern dress, *The Old Adam*, *The Marvellous History of Saint Bernard*, and *Rosmersholm*, with a revival of *The Immortal Hour* thrown in. Chapin's comedy was particularly appropriate for the time. The action is supposed to take place during a heat-wave, and it was produced at the Kings-way in a heat-wave. The scene was on a house-boat on the Thames, and it opened in London during Henley Week. There is no doubt that a great deal depends on the title of the play, and in the name, *The New Morality*, there is perhaps the slightest suggestion of a treatise. For that, or some other reason—more than likely the hot weather—the public did not flock to the theatre, and Chapin's refreshing little comedy was taken off after four weeks.

Gwen Ffrangcon-Davies gave an enchanting performance as Betty, the wife, described by *Punch* as a " lovely, lively study of an intelligent modern woman " in which " she conveyed her author's intention that you should see in her fiery unreason the sweet reason that lay behind it." Cedric Hardwicke was content with the tiny part of a soldier-manservant, and with about twenty lines to speak he succeeded in providing an admirable full-length portrait. Finely in the picture were also Wallace Evennett as the other husband, and Scott Sunderland as Betty's good-natured, solid, rather foolish, spouse.

CHAPTER VI

"HAMLET" IN MODERN DRESS

IT would not be an exaggeration to say that *Hamlet* in modern dress, which was the next production at the Kingsway, is one of the most important things in the stage history of recent years. Not because the experiment was repeated in Vienna, in New York, and afterwards by amateurs in London and elsewhere, but because it has shaken to the foundations the method of staging the "classics." Its influence was felt three years later, for instance, when Harcourt Williams took charge of the productions at the Old Vic, and was criticised—rightly in my opinion—for allowing some of the actors to gabble their speeches to such an extent that not only the poetry but the intelligibility was lost. The Old Vic, under Mr. Williams's skilful directorship, soon found its level, and the next season, when John Gielgud joined the company, a great deal of the traditional way of playing Shakespeare—the slow tempo, the meaningless back-slapping and the archaic "business"—had been dropped. In fact, only the costumes remained to remind us that we were watching a classic.

Looking back it is possible to see Barry Jackson's experiment in its true perspective. To put *Hamlet* in modern dress was only a reversion to the eighteenth century, when plays were normally presented in the costumes of the period. In the Variorum Edition of *Hamlet*, for instance, there is the translation of a letter from G. H. Lichtenberg to a friend on Garrick's performance as Hamlet. It is dated October 1775, and the following is an extract:

"It occurs to me that antique costumes on the stage are to us, if we are not too learned, a sort of masquerade habit, which indeed, if it is handsome, gives us pleasure, but a pleasure so small that it can hardly add to the sum of all else that goes to increase the effect of the piece. . . . I think then, when our modern dress in a play does not offend the sensitive dignity of our scholastic learning, we ought by all means to retain it. Our French dress coats have long since attained to the dignity of a skin, and their folds have the significance of personal traits and expressions, and all the wrestling and bending and fighting and falling in a strange costume we may understand, but we do not feel."

It is easy to forget, when confronted with a print of Garrick as Macbeth in full-skirted coat and knee breeches and Lady Macbeth in hooped skirts, that the actors were not in costume at all, and that the players in Shakespeare's time, in their doublet and hose—in which they almost certainly appeared—were in much the same clothes as those worn by the audience. Not that this in itself is an excuse for putting Hamlet in a lounge suit and the King in a boiled shirt of to-day, for in the last hundred years or so the Hamlet costume has been standardised. It may stand for no particular period, but the clothes are now accepted without question by the audience. The test of a well-dressed man is that nobody notices his clothes; the same test might be applied to a well-dressed Hamlet.

One has only to read the headlines in the newspapers in August 1925 to be reminded that the clothes were of paramount importance in this production. "Hamlet in Plus-fours" was of course the favourite; very few sub-editors could resist it. Other headings were: "Ophelia in a Jumper," "Gloomy Dane with Cigarette," "A Fashion Parade in Hamlet," and "The Jazz Hamlet." News headings do not always represent the tone of a critic's article, and it should be said at once they did not do so in the reviews of the modern-dress production. Speaking generally it was taken as seriously as Barry Jackson intended, and if there were any members of the audience on the first night who came to laugh most of them remained, if not to pray, certainly to be profoundly moved. Barry Jackson was of course as sincere as he has ever been in his life. It was evident that the greatest dramatist of all time was not successful in the theatre and, as a manager who had staged seventeen of the plays in Birmingham, he tried to discover the reason for Shakespeare's unpopularity. Was it owing to our bad production? Was it something that came between the play and the audience? Was it the blank verse? Barry Jackson had asked himself these questions two years before—after acting as adjudicator at a Shakespearean festival for school-children in Birmingham. Several teams had appeared dressed in " the motley," the fairies in art muslin and Christmas-tree ornaments, the others in costumes that accentuated the unreality of the whole thing. Then a band of youngsters appeared in the play scene from *A Midsummer Night's Dream*. They came from a very poor district, and were dressed in their school clothes because they could afford no others. Quince brought his dinner in a red handkerchief and Bottom had borrowed his father's bag of tools. It was a distinct relief after the bath-towels, the nightgowns, the absurd little frocks, and the artificial flowers. The stage suddenly became alive with human beings who acted the comic scene better than the others, because they were not awed and hampered by unfamiliar dresses.

Those Birmingham school-children must have the credit—or blame—for the " modern-dress " productions, for shortly afterwards it was decided to stage *Cymbeline* at the Repertory Theatre, and when the question of the costumes arose, neither Shelving nor Ayliff could decide in which period the play should be dressed. So modern dress was suggested and finally adopted. This experiment had been interesting, if a trifle tentative; it certainly had opened a new approach to Shakespeare, suggesting that if he were treated as a modern dramatist instead of an archaic classic people might go to see the plays. It was necessary to break away somehow from the ordinary presentation of Shakespeare, which produced a feeling of awe and bewilderment in the spectator, who was perpetually reminded by the dresses and the speeches that the play he was watching was three hundred years old and about a set of people who were quite remote from the world of to-day. Barry Jackson therefore took *Hamlet*,

51

the sublimest of the tragedies, and attempted to prove to the man in the street, the ordinary everyday playgoer, that its problems were as real to-day as they were in Shakespeare's day. The play was visualised afresh, approached entirely from the angle of the twentieth century and, of course, it stood the test remarkably well. A year or two before playgoers had been moved by the last act in *The Vortex*, in which a modern young man upbraids his cocktail-drinking mother, and it was possible to see how Shakespeare had anticipated Noel Coward in the closet scene. Perhaps the most striking gain was in the play scene, for then the actors in their mediæval costumes were differentiated from the people of the Court, whereas usually the players wear almost identi-cally the same clothes as the others.

Did the modern-clothes production succeed in its purpose ? Certainly it ran well into November—the longest run of *Hamlet* for a good many years—and it attracted a great deal of attention—more, indeed, than any play of Shakespeare's for generations. It was frankly experimental. The chief criticism that can be brought against the production concerns the speaking of the verse and not the dressing of the play. It is true that the poetry is there and cannot be wholly lost, but, at the same time, great lines, magnificent words, cannot be spoken in the same way as modern colloquialisms. With dress-suits, flannel trousers, bowler hats, and short frocks came a naturalism of speech that meant a loss of beauty to sensitive ears. But more was gained.

For centuries Hamlet had been the greatest of all star parts, the leading man's holiday. In this production the play of *Hamlet* was seen in perspective without the Prince of Denmark being emphasised out of all proportion. The " hand-some, middle-aged gentleman " (to use Ivor Brown's words), indulging in a spate of gentle rhetoric, was replaced by a rebellious young man tortured to the verge of madness. Colin Keith-Johnston was passionately sincere in a way that was stark in its modernity. It was a performance that would have been impossible to imagine in the traditional doublet and hose, and what was

52

lacking in beauty—a good deal of the loveliness of the verse was lost, for instance—was compensated by the rugged virility of the characterisation.

The production (which had the thrill of the first-night of a new play) was remarkably fresh and vivid, and exquisitely patterned. The King and Queen were tragic figures in a very moving drama, and Frank Vosper's smooth, polished, urbane Claudius and Dorothy Massingham's sullen Gertrude certainly let fresh light into the play. For once the line " to smile and be a villain " meant something real, for it was possible to believe that the Queen could have fallen in love with this good-looking King. Polonius was perhaps the biggest gainer. When one recalled the many very boring performances of Shakespeare's creation of a boring old gentleman, Bromley Davenport's neatly bearded, frock-coated, highly amusing, and thoroughly untraditional rendering was in itself a justification of Barry Jackson's experiment. There was an appealing simplicity about the youthful Ophelia presented by Muriel Hewitt. Cedric Hardwicke's bowler-hatted, dry-witted grave-digger was seen to be a near relative of Churdles Ash.

No theatrical event for many years caused so much attention as the modern *Hamlet*, and long descriptive notices of the play appeared in the chief American papers and many of the Continental journals. It was praised in unsuspected quarters. W. B. Yeats was an enthusiastic admirer, and asked Barry Jackson if he would take the whole production to Dublin after the London run. John Galsworthy sent his congratulations, but warned the producer " not to lose his head about it," and William Poel, the founder of the Elizabethan Stage Society, wrote a long letter to the *Manchester Guardian*, in which he said that the Kingsway production " is a record performance in the stage-history of the tragedy, that is to say, it is the first attempt to be made by any producer in modern times to arrange a stage version of the dialogue so as to give prominence to its dominant motive—namely, that of revenge." Gordon Craig, in a light-hearted article in *The Graphic*, after mentioning that he had the same idea in 1904, possibly summed up the truth of the situation when he said that there " is something to be said for performing the Shakespearean drama in modern clothes. And when I say modern clothes, I say modern with a difference : modern in suggestion, not blatantly modern."

The Men's Wear Organiser had something to say about the clothes. The sartorial expert was very upset about the Prince, who was " in the air " in regard to his rig-out. " His evening kit was a sheer disgrace. The soft shirt and soft double collar, worn with a suit which does not appear to be even the correct evening-dress material, are abundant evidence that his mind is just a little deranged." But his plus-fours were admired, and the writer liked " the double-breasted suits worn by Laertes, Horatio, and the *jeunesse dorée* of the Danish Court." *The Tailor and Cutter* also had a word to say on the subject ; suggesting that Hamlet's fondness for a dinner jacket and soft collar when everyone else was in full evening-dress made him look like " a peevish provincial boy, unaware of the etiquette of dress." It is amusing to notice that *The Outfitter*, faced with a production in which " there were few sartorial errors of real importance," criticised the " glaring sartorial mistakes " made by members of the audience, especially a few of the daily paper critics. " In a first night of this nature," the writer complained, " it is hardly the thing to wear an ill-fitting ' dicky,' as one of the gentlemen did." Fortunately, Sir Frank Benson was " elegantly dressed," and Bransby Williams wore a " dinner jacket-suit of excellent cut," and there were other actors present who gave tone to a house that was let-down by the critics !

Punch rose wittily to the occasion with its Raven Hill cartoon—" Measure for Measure "—representing G. B. S. in Elizabethan costume posed in the manner of the familiar statue of Shakespeare talking to the Bard, who was a dapper little figure in trousers and jacket.

Shakespeare : " Hullo, old thing ! What's the idea ? "

Mr. Bernard Shaw : " Well, as you're dressing like that, I thought I'd dress like this."

Generally speaking, the production was praised by the critics, although there were several dissentients. On the following Sunday " Observator " in *The Observer* printed extracts from some of the notices side by side:

" An opening out of fresh light upon the play."—*The Times*.

" The whole spectacle was as in-congruous as any producer could have made it."—*Star*.

" A complete success."—*Daily Tele-graph*.

" The production seemed to me to be almost denuded of beauty."—*Daily News*.

" The completest and perhaps the most triumphant Hamlet of the present generation."—*Daily Chronicle*.

" Neither so funny nor so revealing as it was expected to be."—*Evening Standard*.

" The playgoer will find *Hamlet* a new and living masterpiece."—*West-minster Gazette*.

" No case was made out for modern clothes, or, indeed, for any type of clothes."—*Daily Express*.

He then suggested that " it only remains for someone to try the contrary experiment and produce *Fallen Angels* in Restoration Costume, or *The Wild Duck* as a tragedy of mediæval Italy." It was Hubert Griffith, *The Observer* critic at that time, who came out most strongly on the side of modern dress, publishing a little book, called *Iconoclastes—the Future of Shakespeare*, which he dedicated " to two sporting gentlemen, Sir Barry Jackson and H. K. Ayliff." It was written in a somewhat excited state of mind, for after coming to the false conclusion " that there will be no other way of doing Shakespeare in the future," Mr. Griffith made a " recantation " in the last chapter, and admitted that it does not matter how the plays are dressed, that any method that keeps to the universal spirit of the drama is legitimate:

" The only way that is definitely wrong is to treat them as they are mostly treated at the moment—to invent a special set of symbols, mannerisms, movements, pronunciations, gestures, that are alone imagined to be ' Shakespearean,' and that are alone thought capable of interpreting him to our eyes.   There is nothing that is ' Shakespearean '; and nothing that can be more than human. The plaster idol with his hand to his domed forehead must be torn down, and the man—who was so human and amusing himself—is resurrected in his place."

Nobody will disagree about that !

CHAPTER VII

MORE KINGSWAY PRODUCTIONS—"THE OLD ADAM"—"THE MARVELLOUS HISTORY OF SAINT BERNARD"—"ROSMERSHOLM"

BARRY JACKSON was at the Kingsway until the November of the following year, and in the last twelve months of his season there were four productions, *The Old Adam*, a revival of *The Immortal Hour*, *The Marvellous History of Saint Bernard*, and *Rosmersholm*, as varied and as interesting a selection of plays as it is possible to imagine. An average run of three months is not bad as things go, but it is safe to say that a good deal of money was lost. It needed courage and money to carry on, and Barry Jackson had both, fortunately for the London theatre.

Seventeen years before, in February 1908, Cicely Hamilton had made her reputation as a dramatist at the Kingsway with *Diana of Dobsons*, and it was therefore a happy idea to put on her play, *The Old Adam*, which had been produced under the title of *The Human Factor* at Birmingham the previous year. Like *Diana of Dobsons*, the new piece had some social significance, and it was presented at an appropriate moment. Its theme was the psychology of the war spirit, and the eyes of the world were then on Locarno; but although the play was excellently acted, well received on the first night, and had good notices from the critics, it failed to attract the public in any numbers.

Miss Hamilton treated a profound subject in a light and fantastic manner. It is Mr. Shaw's method, and, apparently, people will not tolerate anybody else following in his footsteps. Or, possibly, they like their Ruritanian plays to be undiluted romance. At this date there is no need to go deeply into Miss Hamilton's modern parable, which opened in the mythical State of Paphlagonia at the moment when war was about to be declared on its aggressive neighbour,

Ruritania. The people of Paphlagonia were pacific and unprepared. It seemed fortunate therefore that a scientific gentleman should come forward with an invention that would paralyse the enemy's mechanical powers. But it appeared that Ruritania had also the secret of the " negative ray," and both countries were left, as it was thought, powerless. But the human element had been overlooked, and the war spirit, once aroused, was not so easily ex-tinguished. The Old Adam, or—as one of the critics suggested, the Old Cain—was uppermost, and if the guns could not be fired, there were scythes and bill-hooks for weapons, and *The Skylark*, under the Admiralty of Joe Bunting, to lead the improvised navy into action.

The satire was directed against the whole community, and neither states-man nor everyday citizen was spared Miss Hamilton's direct but always good-humoured shafts. The play was very amusing; it was also exceedingly wise. These two elements together were evidently too much for the playgoers of 1925, and the piece was withdrawn in January 1926. It was delightfully acted by Fewlass Llewellyn as the pompous Prime Minister, Charles Carson as the dry, flippant War Minister, Scott Sunderland as the confident soldier, William J. Rea as a bishop, and Roy Byford, George Howe, Clifford Marquand, Drelincourt Odlum, and Frances Clare.

The revival of *The Immortal Hour* followed *The Old Adam* on January 30 with practically the same company, and there is little more to record than that one paper described Midir as the " manager" from the spirit world ! The next production was Barry Jackson's own translation of Ghéon's *The Mar-vellous History of Saint Bernard*, one of the most beautiful things seen on the London stage in our time. Since 1929 the Malvern Festival has been very successfully instituted with G. B. S. as its patron saint, and it is necessary to say at once that the St. Bernard of the title is not the sage of Whitehall Court, but the founder of the famous monastery in Switzerland. It is possible that *The Marvellous History* has brought more pleasure to Barry Jackson than any-thing with which he has been connected in the theatre. The finding of the

58

Costume Design for a Devil
in
"The Marvellous History of Saint Bernard"

play, the subsequent friendship with Ghéon, and his satisfaction with the lovely settings in which Paul Shelving caught the whole spirit of the mediæval mystery, were something outside the ordinary range of production. Barry Jackson, when motoring in Switzerland in August 1924, went out of his way to visit a sick friend in Zurich. There he read in a local newspaper a notice of the representation of a French mystery to celebrate the millenary of St. Bernard of Menthon. This was something after his own heart, and hurrying across to Savoy he discovered, after a good deal of difficulty, that the play was being given in the grounds of the Château de Menthon, near Annecy. He finally succeeded in getting a seat, and was so impressed by the simple beauty of the play which was acted by local people, that he immediately took steps to acquire the rights of translation.

The performance had been arranged by the Count of Menthon, and the young count took the part of his famous ancestor. The family possessed the manuscript of the mystery, which was inscribed on the parchment cover in eighteenth-century handwriting as " Partie du Livre Manuscrit de la Vie de S. Bernard de Menthon." It had been adapted, at the request of the Count, by Henri Ghéon, the distinguished French poet who was then only known to a few discriminating people in this country. The original mystery was probably written in the fifteenth century, and was based to some extent on the life of the saint in the Acta Sanctorum. Ghéon's version preserved the devout simplicity of the early play, and Barry Jackson made an inspired translation which was effective on the stage. The piece had rhythmical beauty, and it was good stuff for the actors to speak. He made certain necessary alterations, however, for the London production. In M. Ghéon's play Christ is enthroned in Heaven together with Our Lady, the Archangel Gabriel, and St. Nicholas, but as the English law forbids the representation of Our Lord on the stage, the speeches attributed to Him were given to Our Lady. As Barry Jackson stated in the preface to the published version, this was at first misunderstood by Catholics. He pointed out that the language of the Heavenly characters assumes the unseen presence of the Divine Majesty whom they supplicate on man's behalf.

Bernard of Menthon is one of the most popular of saints. He founded the famous hospice on the top of the pass that bears his name, and his dogs—which were probably introduced into the monastery centuries later, for they are not mentioned in the mediæval play—are known all over the world. But most people were not familiar with the legend of the heir of the house of Menthon, who renounced his lovely young bride on the night before his marriage and, under the guidance of St. Nicholas, entered a religious community. Later, when he had become an archdeacon, Bernard determined to overthrow the devil who demands a tithe of the bands of pilgrims crossing the Alps on their way to Rome. In order to accomplish his Heaven-sent mission, Bernard takes his place as tenth man in the Pilgrimage, sends the hosts of Satan helter-skelter to the nether regions, and leaves the road to Rome freed for ever from devilish domination.

In his setting Paul Shelving represented very decoratively the three dimen-sions of the Middle Ages. The stage was the world in which St. Bernard lived, and the scenes were laid in his father's castle, and in the monastery of Aosta. Framed above the alcove in the centre was a Fra Angelico Heaven with the Madonna crowned and enthroned between the winged St. Gabriel and the mitred and croziered St. Nicholas, and below, in the orchestra well, were the nether regions where dwelt Satan and his hosts of devils.

Pictorially, the setting resembled a very beautiful illuminated missal, for Shelving had captured some of the glory of the Primitive painter's vision. Practically, it showed what could be done to produce a play in which the scenes were set on the earth, in the sky, and in the world beneath on a small stage that did not revolve and lacked rollers and bridges and all the other inventions that are supposed to be indispensable to theatre artists to-day. The effect was a thing of exquisite beauty, although a few people objected to the mediæval crudeness of the devils, who sported realistically at times in the stalls.

60

In the early manner the audience was brought into intimate touch with the stage, and the production by A. E. Filmer (who had also directed the rehearsals of the original performance at Birmingham during H. K. Ayliff's absence abroad) revealed throughout a true sense of period, carefully altered to the somewhat artificial requirements of a modern theatre. Ernest Irving in his arrangement of the music did not attempt to find material in contemporary sources; but his selections—scored for two oboes, two bassoons, and harp— had a charming appropriateness.

There was universal agreement about the acting. Few people who saw the play will forget Valerie Taylor's celestial loveliness as the Queen of Heaven, realising, according to Hubert Griffith (one of the few critics who did not like the production), the beauty of Botticelli's Madonna of the Magnificat. Denys Blakelock as St. Gabriel, and Grosvenor North as St. Nicholas, were gracious figures from an illuminated book of saints. Robert Harris conveyed superbly the ascetic fervour of the youthful Bernard, who became the patron saint of all travellers, and there was delicate poise and understanding in Gwen Ffrangcon-Davies's study of the young bride. H. O. Nicholson seemed to radiate the spirit of devotion as the old Prior of Aosta; James Dale, Dennis Barry, and George Howe leavened the "history" with some vigorous humour; and Scott Sunderland and Margaret Chatwin were excellent as Bernard's parents.

Henri Ghéon attended the first performance in London, and made a short speech in French at the end of the evening. It was Barry Jackson's first meeting with the poet, who also came over to see his *Demos, King and Slave* at the Arts Theatre last year.

The Marvellous History of Saint Bernard remained at the Kingsway until June 12, 1926, but it would have run for a longer time and been a financial success if it had not been hit by the general strike. It was succeeded by a short run of *Rosmersholm*, with Edith Evans as Rebecca West. The version was specially made by F. Farquharson Sharp for this production, and it

61

differed somewhat from the translation which is included in the Everyman Library edition. The characters talked a language that sounded like colloquial English; one recognised the fresh note as soon as the curtain rose and Rebecca West told the housekeeper to " close the window." The familiar figures in Ibsen's great tragic drama were in modern clothes, and the setting in a " manor-house " was delocalised. The gaunt-looking Scandinavian stove, the prominent feature of the usual Ibsen production, was missing, and, acting on the theory that to British playgoers characters with foreign names are not human beings, Ulrick Brendel became Eric Brendon, the editor of *The Searchlight* was called Alfred Robinson, and Mrs. Helseth appeared as Martha. These changes were happier than the transformation of Kroll, who was acclimatised as James Crowley. His diehard views—or at any rate the expression of them —hardly seemed to fit the smartly dressed grammar-school master, despite the exceedingly good performance of Rupert Harvey in a part that must always be an ungrateful one for an actor.

Rebecca West, on the other hand, is one of the most magnificent parts ever written. It is so much bigger than life that there are few actresses who can tackle the character, which is no doubt the reason why the play is so rarely staged. Someone of the calibre of Edith Evans is needed, and this superb artist achieved one of the triumphs of her career in the Kingsway production. Rebecca West was pitilessly unveiled before the audience, and the actress expressed every mood and laid bare the subtlest gradation of feeling. The tortured self-analytical scenes with Rosmer were perfectly rendered, and the character grew with the play, the quiet still moments contrasting vividly with the rising tide of passion. It is a criticism of our theatre that Miss Evans's performance in H. K. Ayliff's production was seen only for a few weeks at the Kingsway and then forgotten: whereas in any other country in Europe it would have passed into the repertory of a National Theatre. Charles Carson acted well, although he was not too happily cast as Rosmer; and Robert Farquharson, in a make-up which was described by James Agate as a " Christmas-party idea of Walt Whitman," was effective as Brendon, particularly in the second act. Muriel Aked's neatly studied housekeeper, and George Howe's socialist editor completed the company.

Rosmersholm ended this adventurous and highly experimental season, which should have been continued with a production of *The Master Builder* and possibly another play if Horace Watson had not asked Barry Jackson to present *Yellow Sands* at very short notice at the Haymarket Theatre.

CHAPTER VIII

MORE PHILLPOTTS—" YELLOW SANDS "—" THE BLUE COMET "—" THE RUNAWAYS "—" THE MAYOR "—" DEVONSHIRE CREAM "—" JANE'S LEGACY "

A MONTH or two before *The Farmer's Wife* ended its run of nearly three years *Yellow Sands* was presented at the Haymarket by Barry Jackson in association with Horace Watson. It was one of the happiest and most successful associations in the history of the modern theatre, for the play—this time a collaboration between Eden Phillpotts and his daughter Adelaide—was generally considered a good deal better-made, and, at the same time, quite as amusing as its famous prototype at the Court. The critics were unanimous in their commendation; in fact, the only disgruntled notice appeared in *The Nation*, the writer admitting at the same time that he was " hardly the right person to criticise *Yellow Sands*" as he was "too exasperated by life . . . to appreciate properly what is known as ' harmless fun,' particularly when ' rustics ' are the topic." The others, with a friendlier outlook on life, enjoyed themselves very much, and one dramatic critic was seen loudly applauding at the end of the long evening !

Yellow Sands had been submitted to Frederic Harrison, the lessee of the Haymarket, shortly before he died in June 1926, and, although he liked the play, he said he saw no prospect of producing it for some time. It was then acquired by Barry Jackson, who some time in October 1926, less than six months after Harrison's death, received a message from Horace Watson asking him if he could produce *Yellow Sands* at once. This meant a great deal of intensive work for the company. H. K. Ayliff rushed down to Devonshire with the script and suggestions for certain alterations in the construction of

65

the play. He arrived early one morning and Eden Phillpotts, who is a very quick worker, rewrote several scenes before lunch. Cyril Phillips was already on the spot, and he and Paul Shelving went off in a car and visited *Yellow Sands*, breathed the atmosphere of the fishing village for a few hours, called at several of the cottages, and had tea, afterwards going on to Salcombe, where they purchased a boat, some crab-pots, and other properties to be sent to London. In the meantime the company had been engaged, within a day or two rehearsals had begun, and *Yellow Sands* opened on November 3, 1926, less than three weeks later. Cedric Hardwicke, Ralph Richardson, and Muriel Hewitt were playing in *Devonshire Cream* on tour when the rehearsals began, and they travelled up from Eastbourne every day.

Again the plot was of little account. The theme has some slight affinity with *Jane's Legacy*, which had a brief run in Birmingham and was afterwards to be seen at the Duchess Theatre. Instead of the inland Devonshire village, the Phillpotts had gone to the sea-coast and given a series of portraits of the inhabitants of *Yellow Sands*. There were Jenifer Varwell, the charming old lady of eighty with a tidy bit of money to leave, and the relations and friends who expected to be remembered in her will. Among the claimants were the delightful, wine-bibbing old reprobate, Richard Varwell, whose philosophy was summed up in the line: " Let them who can't dream, work "; the bitter-tongued rapacious sister Mary; the pleasant young nephew, and the fiery socialistic crab-fisher, Joe Varwell, who eventually inherited the residue of the estate and turned Conservative. The story was simple enough, but the character-drawing was better than in *The Farmer's Wife*, because it was a trifle nearer to life. Few will forget Cedric Hardwicke's performance as Richard Varwell, an entirely different creation from Churdles Ash, and it must be remembered that between the two plays he had appeared as Cæsar in *Cæsar and Cleopatra*, a manservant in *The New Morality*, and the first grave-digger in *Hamlet*. Also in the company were Susan Richmond as the old lady; Frank Vosper (later to add to his reputation as a playwright), as

66

the defiant young rebel against social order, a part that was in severe contrast with his sardonic King in the modern *Hamlet*; Ralph Richardson as a breezy young lover; H. O. Nicholson, Drusilla Wills and her sister, Muriel Hewitt, Viola Lyel, Edward Petley, and Amy Veness. It was hardly a smart Haymarket cast, yet the play ran for 612 performances, and when it was withdrawn on February 25, 1928, wanted only five more to beat the record for the theatre, then held by *Bunty Pulls the Strings* with 617 performances. Both figures have since been eclipsed by St. John Ervine's *The First Mrs. Fraser*.

It was a triumph for H. K. Ayliff, the producer, who handled his company of actors as a team, and he was fortunate, as someone said at the O.P. Club *Yellow Sands* dinner, in having " a team without a tail." Eden Phillpotts never saw the play, but he paid a tribute to the company in a letter:

" Nobody can do anything on earth single-handed, except make a fool of himself; and none, at every step, depends more than the dramatist on his fellow men and women. To them he must look for every living value his work may possess. Without them he cannot live at all, and their gracious will has made many a doubtful babe grow up into a pleasing child."

Altogether Barry Jackson has produced in London six plays by the Phillpotts, two of which were enormous successes and the other four fairly complete failures. Certainly the gains on the swings made up for the losses on the roundabouts, of which *The Blue Comet*, the more serious-minded comedy that had to face the ordeal of following *The Farmer's Wife* at the Court, was perhaps the most sensational. The play opened on February 23, 1927, and it was off before the end of March.

It is difficult to account for so complete a failure, for most people would have hazarded that the author's name under a play at the Court would have been sufficient draw to keep the piece going for several months, especially when it is remembered that *Yellow Sands* was filling the Haymarket. But in the theatre news travels almost as fast as Mr. Phillpotts's comet and it was rapidly known that this was another kind of Phillpotts. Having once, like Arnold Bennett's artist, made a reputation for "painting pictures of policemen blowing whistles," the public expected him to go on "painting pictures of policemen blowing whistles." To forsake Devonshire for artistic circles in Hampstead and then to introduce a devastating comet needed some adjustment of mental attitude, and the crowds who had flocked to *The Farmer's Wife* stayed away from *The Blue Comet*.

At the same time it must be admitted that the play was not too satisfactory. The author had treated his plot—which was about as big a theme as it is possible to imagine—in a somewhat off-hand fashion. He started one hare in the first act, the visit of the wealthy and unconventional Australian to the conventional Bedale Family, and later dragged in the comet which was to destroy the earth on a date fixed by a Royal Commission. And the brusque young visitor from the Antipodes was more interesting than the destroyer from the sky—"All of which," as Edith Shackleton wittily said, "was rather a waste of a good comet."

The Australian was played by Paul Cavanagh, a young actor who had joined the Birmingham Repertory Theatre the previous year. It was a re-freshingly virile performance, which would have carried a better play to success. There were clever character-sketches by George Elton, Dorothy Hall, and Clarence Blakiston; and Barry Jackson's niece, Cecily Byrne, who as a child had appeared at The Grange in a performance of Foote's comedy, *The Lyar*, as long ago as 1903, acted the part of Millicent Bedale. It was generally admitted that *The Blue Comet* was extremely well acted, and finely set by Paul Shelving.

Next on the Phillpotts list was *The Runaways*, which was put on at the Garrick Theatre on November 14, 1928, where it followed Basil Dean's successful production of *The Constant Nymph*, and, although Eden Phillpotts was again back in Devonshire in rustic surroundings, the play failed to attract audiences, and was speedily withdrawn. The truth is, the author had been seen at his best in *Yellow Sands,* and unless he could provide something as entertaining in the same *genre* the public made up its mind to give the play a miss.   The characters were extravagantly farcicalised versions of stage-types that had now become familiar : Matthew Borlase, suspected of an intrigue with an unknown woman because he suddenly assumes habits of thriftiness ; his loutish son, with suicidal ideas because he is jilted in favour of a commercial traveller ; the daughter, in revolt because her father will not consent to her marriage with a hired man ; Mrs. Borlase, " a mountain of flesh to fill the eyes of Rubens " (to quote James Agate), who plans an elopement with a ludicrous vegetarian lover ; the old " Granfer," an anæmic edition of Churdles Ash and Richard Varwell ; and the inevitable spinster—always a figure of fun in Eden Phillpotts's eyes—this time with corns.   One can leave it at that, and say that Sam Livesey, H. O. Nicholson, Ben Field, Dorothy Hall, Colin Keith-Johnston, Eileen Beldon, Muriel Hewitt, and Ralph Richardson put their best into the comedy.

A play was required in the spring of 1929 to follow *Bird in Hand* at the Royalty Theatre, and it was decided to put on *The Mayor,* a comedy that had been written by Adelaide Phillpotts without the help of her father.   It was produced on March 11 and withdrawn on March 23, 1929.   Miss Phillpotts set out with an interesting idea which she failed to manage quite as well as it deserved.   If it was anything the play was a study in the repressions that no doubt exist in an average respectable seaside resort.   The Phillpotts usually indulge in tea-parties, and in *The Mayor* there are three, one in each act. They served the definite purpose of bringing the élite of Westhaven together for critical gossip.   In the first act the party is arranged to meet the Mayor, a well-drawn study of a self-made man who was beautifully played by William Heilbronn, the actor who had just taken the part in Birmingham.   At the end there is the first of the tea-cup brainstorms, for the Mayor, exasperated beyond all control by a snobbish and obstinate retired Admiral, who had baited and bullied him throughout the afternoon, grabs a cake-knife and tries

69

to stab the dreadful old gentleman. This primitive outburst has the effect of unloosing the emotions of the other residents as the tea-parties that follow serve to show. Although Miss Phillpotts did not handle her material to the best advantage, some of the side-lights on the life that is led in the genteel towns with esplanades were vigorously robust satire, and there was some excellent characterisation, a good deal of which was allowed to run to seed.

The production suffered on the opening night through the absence from the cast of Dorothy Hall, who was taken ill a few hours before the curtain rose. She had the important part of the vinegar-tongued old woman who served as a cross-grained chorus, and at Birmingham she had held the play together. It was absolutely necessary for a smooth performance that this part should be well played. The understudy was not ready and another actress had to go on with a script in her hand. It is therefore fairly certain that Miss Phillpotts was blamed for faults that were due to Miss Hall's unfortunate illness. The other characters were acted for all their worth, and the performances of Eileen Beldon as Bertha Beck, O.B.E., the strident feminist, Isabel Thornton as a wealthy vulgarian, and Cicely Oates as the spinster hostess, stand out clearly in the long and heterogeneous company.

Barry Jackson had agreed to do a number of Phillpotts plays, and for a long time he had waited for the opportunity of putting on *Devonshire Cream* in London with Cedric Hardwicke in the part he had played on tour, but the chance never came. Early in 1930, after the failure of *The White Assegai*, a play was wanted for the Playhouse, and Eden Phillpotts's comedy was staged with Horace Hodges in what can appropriately be called the Hardwicke part of William Blee. One can say this without disrespect to that charming and very experienced actor, for the creator of Churdles Ash and Richard Varwell was the obvious choice for Blee, the more genial old labourer who was such a near relation. There is no need to say that Horace Hodges gave a delicious performance, " as lovable as an aged apple-tree" as James Agate said in the *Sunday Times*. But although the play had a fair run it was a losing battle most of the time. It certainly lost money, despite the fact that Mr. Phillpotts was back in his own country.

The story was a very trumpery affair. Two households in fair "Darty-moor" bear each other an ancient grudge, and the author—lacking Shakespeare's tragic conviction—provided a story of considerably less woe than that of Juliet and her Romeo. After three wordy acts, in which Elias Widecombe—the Devonshire Montague—repeats himself a great deal, it is found that Robert Blanchard, the Romeo in the case (in love, of course, with Widecombe's daughter), is not really a Blanchard at all, a very unworthy subterfuge to bring about a happy ending. Again the "pastoral clown" came to the rescue, but without succeeding in saving the play. The evening was pleasant while Mr. Hodges was on the stage pointing out to his master the absurdity of carrying on the feud—"what's the good of hating a tree because last year's plums gave you a belly-ache." Sam Livesey battled manfully with the part of the sententious farmer, and Mary Jerrold was the soul of graciousness as the farmer's wife and the mother of the Devonshire Juliet, who was attractively played by Phyllis Shand. Harry Wilcoxon made an excellent impression upon the first-night audience (which included Bernard Shaw) as the youthful lover—"ill starred" until the final ten minutes—and H. O. Nicholson presented rusticity in its second childhood. Possibly because they were becoming a trifle tired of the "mixture as before," the critics were not too friendly to *Devonshire Cream*, and Gladys Cooper had a bone to pick with Alan Parsons of the *Daily Mail* about his notice.

"In these days of endeavour to protect struggling industries from unfair attack," she said, in her letter to the editor, "cannot critics, while retaining perfect freedom in their critical capacity, be prevented from doing damage to the theatre by advertising their purely personal views and omitting to give a fair representation of the effect of the play upon its audience ?

"Last night I attended the first night of *Devonshire Cream*, by Eden

Phillpotts. As shown by the success of *The Farmer's Wife* and *Yellow Sands*, there are many thousands of playgoers who greatly appreciate Mr. Phillpotts's work, of which this is a typical sample.

" Your critic apparently does not. I can understand, therefore, that he did not enjoy his evening.

" However, it is quite obvious, from the marked attention of the audience and from the applause which greeted every line of comedy, that many hundreds of Mr. Phillpotts's admirers who were there thoroughly enjoyed themselves.

" Your critic contented himself with writing a disgruntled account of his own personal reactions to the play and gave no impression whatsoever of the general appreciation of the audience.

" Thus he has doubtless been the means of preventing a number of people from seeing this excellent play.

" By all means let critics criticise, but let them also give a fair representation of what the public thinks of the play."

Alan Parsons in his reply pointed out that the " general appreciation of a first-night audience is, to a large extent, an artificial one," and that he was sent to a theatre to present his own personal views and not those of the people sitting to the right or left of him. Then Dame Laura Knight entered into the fray, and said that in her opinion Mr. Parsons's notice was incomplete and one-sided, for *Devonshire Cream* was obviously a comedy that the public would be glad to see. But perhaps Edgar Wallace's contribution to the controversy was the most pertinent. He wrote :

" It is very amusing to read Miss Cooper's attack on Mr. Alan Parsons for his failure to record the reaction of enthusiasm of the first night of *Devon-shire Cream*.

" I do not know how Miss Cooper can speak with such authority about the attitude of the audience. I have the impression that she left the theatre after the first act ; certainly her seat in the theatre was vacant."

Gladys Cooper admitted that "domestic reasons" had taken her away from the theatre after the first act, but that she flattered herself that she could judge the feelings of a first-night audience.

The theatre papers had leading articles on the subject and *Truth* took the opportunity to agree with Miss Cooper's protest against the egotism of dramatic critics. "Lewd critics of the baser sort should imitate Mr. Charles Morgan, by far the ablest man now writing on the theatre, who, when he himself dislikes a play, never fails to state if the audience thought differently."

But even this row did not turn *Devonshire Cream* into another *Farmer's Wife*, and the play was withdrawn on March 29, 1930.

Louise Hampton made a joke in her speech at the end of *Jane's Legacy*, which was produced at the Duchess Theatre on December 16, 1930. She said that Eden Phillpotts was "writing a play on new lines—something with a tea-party in the plot." But in *Devonshire Cream* the author had departed from his usual stand-by and omitted a party. True; a supper party was mentioned, but it took place between the second and third acts. There was certainly a tea-party in *Jane's Legacy*. It was a lovely party, with the characters in the costumes of a hundred years ago, in the charming garden designed by Paul Shelving, and it was given by Jane Mortimore in order that her friends and relations should share her enjoyment of the legacy of £1,000, which had come as a bolt from the blue. The village of Godbold's Leigh was all agog with excitement and everybody offered advice. A swaggering, roystering sergeant wanted to marry her, and Jane, although not a bit in love with him, flutteringly said "yes"; then her pretty niece's love-affair went wrong, and everything else seemed to go awry because of the unexpected fortune. Before it was discovered that Jane's legacy was not meant for her at all, the poor bewildered creature had come to the conclusion that money was indeed the root of all evil, and the relief of the burden was welcomed with open arms. An unsophisticated story, but in many ways it was the best Phillpotts in London since *Yellow Sands*. Setting the clock back a century was a good notion, for which H. K. Ayliff was responsible. It gave a greater sense of reality to the simply conceived characters. Louise Hampton brought all her charm and sensitiveness to the chief character, and the acting by Frank Pettingell, Viola Lyel, Colin Keith-Johnston, Frank Moore, Harry Caine, Barbara Gott, and Kathleen Harrison can be recalled with relish.

Jane's Legacy had a fairly long run at the Duchess, and if it could have been given only at matinées it would have made a good profit. The afternoon performances were increased to three a week during the run, and they were always full of visitors from the country. London, by this time, seemed to have lost its taste for the wholesome and simple-minded fare that was served up by the Phillpotts. Perhaps Barry Jackson had given them a trifle too much of it. There is such a thing as satiety.

CHAPTER IX

"THE DESPERATE LOVERS"—"BERT'S GIRL"

FOR a few days at the beginning of November 1926 Barry Jackson had three plays running in London: *The Farmer's Wife* at the Court, *Yellow Sands* at the Haymarket, and *Rosmersholm* at the Kingsway. *Rosmersholm* was withdrawn, however, on November 13, and the next production was the ill-fated presentation of Alfred Sutro's comedy *The Desperate Lovers* at the Comedy on January 28, 1927, which was one of the most complete failures of Barry Jackson's career. The comedy was universally "slated" by the press and ran for only a few nights. It might be described as a piece of bad judgment. Really it is another instance of the difficulty of assessing the box-office appeal of a play until the first night. It read well (although this, it must be admitted at once, is no criterion of a play's likelihood of success), and the author was a dramatist of great reputation; the casting was carefully done and one of our greatest comediennes, Irene Vanbrugh, had a leading part; and Paul Shelving's settings were deliciously in the key of the piece. H. K. Ayliff produced the play skilfully enough, but it was more than he or the company could do to save the last tedious act. For Mr. Sutro dangled his quartet of marionettes on their strings until his arm tired, and he was unable to maintain the extravagance of situation to the end.

It is possible that the taste for artificial comedy has been lost, but it is difficult to maintain this in the face of the success of Noel Coward and the popularity of the revivals of *The Way of the World* and *The Beaux' Stratagem*. Mr. Coward is completely of our own times and his characters are based on reality, whereas Mr. Sutro's were artificial figments remote from any other world than the theatre, the stratagems employed by his beaux and belles were as remote

75

from current fashion as anything Farquhar imagined. His Baroness Della Rocca was not a twentieth-century Millamant, nor did Mr. Duminy succeed in establishing the importance of being Alexander !

The story revolved round a preposterous will, a subject beloved of the lesser nineteenth-century playwrights and unworthy of Mr. Sutro. Alexander Duminy and his stepson, Everard Bassopp, had each been left £5,000 a year on the condition that, if they wanted to marry, it was necessary to obtain the other's consent to the alliance. The earlier attempts to fulfil the conditions had failed, and Mr. Seed, the lawyer, had cheerfully drawn the hundred guineas from the estate as his fee for the arbitration. On the present occasion Mr. Duminy wanted to marry the Baroness Della Rocca, and Everard Bassopp the delightful Lady Eulalie Havers. A meeting was arranged, but the affair had again to be left to Mr. Seed. The final dénouement is as absurd as the will itself. The dialogue was highly epigrammatical and there were many amusing lines, but the whole thing was too fantastic for everyday consumption, despite Irene Vanbrugh's gay, light-hearted performance as the Baroness, Allan Aynesworth's polished comedy as Alexander Duminy, Marda Vanne's fresh vitality and her exquisite sense of the ridiculous as Lady Eulalie, and Scott Sunderland's amusingly pompous portrait of the other member of the quartet of desperate lovers.

The first production to follow *The Farmer's Wife* was *The Blue Comet*, which has been dealt with in the chapter on the Phillpotts's plays, and the presentation of *Bert's Girl* by Elizabeth Baker on March 30, 1927, temporarily finished Barry Jackson's season at the Court, although his company returned to that theatre the following year. Miss Baker was one of the discoveries of the Frohman-Granville Barker repertory season, in which her play, *Chains*, had one of the longest runs. It was due to Edward Knoblock's encourage-ment that she had written it, and owing to his interest that the play was originally produced by the Play Actors, a Sunday Society which did a great deal of useful experimental work and has now ceased to exist. A. E. Drinkwater helped her a good deal, and had produced another of her plays called *Partnership* at the Court Theatre.

Despite her success before the war Elizabeth Baker was a great deal better known in the provincial repertory theatres than in London. Barry Jackson had done several of her plays in Birmingham, and the people who remembered *Chains* looked forward with some zest to *Bert's Girl*, the title of which promised another faithful picture of lower-middle-class life. The promise was fulfilled, but the fashion in playgoing had been changed by the glamour of the pictures. Fulham Road and Brixton, the suburban parlour and the Lancashire kitchen, were no longer popular in the theatre, and what chance had Miss Baker with a story about a Cockney family against Frederick Lonsdale and Noel Coward ? Perhaps she realised this and over-emphasised the characterisation in her presentation of the Walters family. H. K. Ayliff also allowed the actors to stress the vulgarity in order to heighten the contrast between Bert and the lovely girl to whom he had been engaged. The company played for laughs a trifle too obviously—a fault that was a virtue in the case of *The Farmer's Wife*. At the same time, the girl should have had Dorothy Black's simple dignity without the utter refinement of voice that from the outset made an alliance with Bert and his dreadful family an impossible thought. It is difficult to apportion the blame between the authoress, the production, and the actors.

This is an attempt to account for the failure of what was very nearly a fine play, for *Bert's Girl* was about something, and, except for the tendency to exaggerate, the characters had some resemblance to reality. They were treated satirically and heightened for theatrical purposes ; it was the Walters in the parlour versus pure beauty represented by the Venus de Milo in the attic upstairs. Life downstairs was set against a background of salmon pink and roses and over the mantelpiece was an overmantel, " a miracle of tiers, idle tiers " (as James Agate put it). The party had been arranged to meet Stella Marsh, the girl that Bert met on his holiday at Margate, whose simplicity of dress and manner brought sneers and sniffs and the usual giggles from his relations. Then Uncle Martin, the aggressive eccentric, stepped into the pande-monium. He was the skeleton in the attic, the old gentleman whose bachelor apartments were filled with beautiful things. To him Stella was Hebe, the handmaiden of the gods, and his eugenic creed revolted against the idea that Stella should mate with Bert and breed another family of vulgar-minded Walters. " And Hebe fell in love with a toad ! Nature, Nature be damned !" he murmured, and the Walters could not answer back, for the house belonged to him.

It was a modern version of Beauty and the Beast, and if one's sympathies were often with the Beast, it was because the part of Bert was played by Henry Caine, whose buoyant and charming personality was there to remind us that possibly vulgarity is eradicable. It was a mean trick to make him drunk, and although Stella made a half-hearted fight to protect her man, who was more victim than villain, it was a losing fight, and odds were laid on the handsome, muscular, and æsthetic young clergyman as soon as he appeared on the scene.

This is not the place to discuss whether, eugenically speaking, the idea was sound, but the play was provocative, and a great deal of it was vivid and entertaining. One would like to see it again with Cedric Hardwicke as Uncle Martin. At the Court the members of the Walters family were highly theatricalised, with Minnie Rayner, Nadine March (as the particularly vulgar-minded younger daughter), and A. J. Denton, Phyllis Percy, Marjorie Lar-combe, and Madge Trenchard in other parts. Edward Chapman, who has since made a name for himself in *The Good Companions*, gave great distinction to the small part of Edgar Tatt.

CHAPTER X

ANOTHER EXPERIMENTAL VENTURE—"THE ADDING MACHINE"—"MACBETH" IN KHAKI

A T the end of the run of *Bert's Girl*, Barry Jackson gave up active management at the Court Theatre and did not resume the control until the following year, when on January 9, 1928, he started another experimental season. The intention was to put on five plays, each of which, whether it was a success or a failure, was to run a month. Unlike many such schemes the original plan did not lapse with the second production, but was carried out to the letter. It was another courageous venture to widen the scope of the theatre; to give London playgoers an idea of the sort of fare that Birmingham had enjoyed for many years. To open with Elmer Rice's expressionist drama, *The Adding Machine*, was a challenge to convention, for this kind of play had hitherto been mainly confined to the producing societies. It had been first produced in London four years before by the Stage Society, with Brember Wills as Mr. Zero and Edith Evans as the clerk who was his opposite cipher in the industrial machine, and had since that date been performed in the repertory theatres throughout the country.

Expressionism is now dead. It has replaced neither the naturalistic play nor the rhetorical drama, but the method, which was born in Germany at the end of the war, expressed the chaos of the time when man was Zero, and it has had a certain vitalising influence on the theatre, as one realised when O'Neill's *Strange Interlude* was seen in London. Expressionism does not wear well. Kaiser's *From Morn to Midnight* was arresting when it was first presented here, but at the second hearing, with the novelty worn off, the inherent faults of the method were too obviously exposed. Character—and not

79

a synthetic rendering of universal type—is still the basis for drama, which is the reason that one can see *Hamlet* twenty times and find fresh things in the play at the twenty-first. There is nothing more to discover in either Mr. Zero in *The Adding Machine* or the Cashier in *From Morn to Midnight* at the second visit. But both plays are worth doing once, and Barry Jackson gave the general public a chance of seeing an example of the modernistic drama before it became as old-fashioned as hobble skirts. He then proceeded to put on *Macbeth* to prove that a play written three hundred years ago was as vital in 1928 as when it was first written.

It is a curious thing that all expressionist dramas deal with the same subject, and start from the same false premise that people who work at machine-made jobs have machine-like minds. Mr. Zero was not a separate individual. He was supposed to be Everyman who sits opposite the same eternal ledger-clerk day by day checking the same eternal invoices while he thinks the same eternally depressing thoughts. In reality, of course, ledger-clerks differ as much from each other as dukes or engine-drivers. Mr. Rice (who has since written in *Street Scene* a play not concerned with type but with character) made the mistake of following Mr. Universal Zero into the next world, whereas the other expressionists gave him up when he quitted this existence. There was little hope in Elysia, although one was grateful for the felicitous respite before Mr. Zero reassumed the slave-like habits of earth. It was an unendurable deterministic philosophy that the author preached. The poor wretched " symbol " was sent to the Cosmic laundry to be cleaned up for another birth and another experience of slavery—which was illogical and unfair treatment for a man who had had the pluck to kill his tyrannical employer ! Murder is not a virtue, but at least it is hardly typical of the slave-mind.

The Adding Machine is a producer's rather than an actor's play, and W. G. Fay, who had directed it in Birmingham, took charge at the Court. Hugh Owen (a young theatre artist who had done brilliant work in Birmingham

Costume Design for a Member of the Cabinet
in
" The Apple Cart "

and has since died) designed some highly stylised settings, suggesting at once that the action was on the abstract plane. Unfortunately, however, the acting was too often on the naturalistic plane. Perhaps it is too much to ask a whole company to assume the mechanical habits of Robots, although in the scene in which the formalised chorus of Mr. One and Mr. Two appeared the effect was startling. The best performance was given by Carrie Baillie, whose mask-like Mrs. Zero succeeded in matching the triangular stage fittings.

Altogether Barry Jackson has been responsible for five modern-dress productions of Shakespeare: *Cymbeline*, *All's Well that Ends Well*, *Hamlet*, *Macbeth*, and *The Taming of the Shrew*, the last three having been seen in London. All were highly experimental in the sense that they constituted an entire break with the tradition of the last two centuries, and, as Barry Jackson said after the first night of *Macbeth* on February 6, 1928, " experiments have their failures." This was one of them, and the people who found most to admire in the *Hamlet* were quick to recognise that there are limitations in the attempt to bring Shakespeare up-to-date.

What was the trouble ? It was partly the dress itself and more certainly the casting of the play. The whole atmosphere of *Macbeth* is mediæval. It is possible to imagine the Thane of Cawdor encountering some witches on a blasted heath, but by no stretch of imagination could it be conceived that a " brass hat " would be likely to do so or, if he did, that he would take any notice of their gabbling. Khaki uniforms have their own definite twentieth-century associations of horror, but the sight of them on the stage in *Macbeth* induced not pity and terror but laughter. It can now be stated that H. K. Ayliff, the producer, had a good deal of difficulty in casting *Macbeth*. Several actors were approached, but they were engaged, and it was offered to Eric Maturin, who is an excellent actor in a suitable part, but was entirely miscast for one that contains some of the loveliest verse ever given to an actor to speak. It is said that Mr. Maturin had never seen the play on the stage; it does not matter much whether he had or not; certainly he fought shy of the poetry and by doing so robbed the play of its greatest quality. Macbeth is a great tragic character by reason of the magnificent things he says, not because of the things he does. Even if the lines had been spoken by an actor who had been trained to speak verse, to give the full value to the words, one doubts whether *Macbeth* would have convinced the audience that the characters in the play thought and acted as people do to-day. Modern staff-officers do not suffer twinges about " incarnadining the multitudinous seas," nor do they talk about " heaven peeping through the blanket of the dark," or think in terms of the " temple-haunting martlet." More's the pity, no doubt.

There were things to admire, however. The blasted heath with its ruined wind-mill silhouetted against the sky and the intermittent machine-gun fire cleverly set the key to this modernised history of " old, unhappy, far-off things." As soon as Mary Merrall read the letter as Lady Macbeth one realised that her costume did not matter very much. She superseded the dress, and spoke the lines not only with a feeling for the rhythm but as if they meant something. In the sleep-walking scene she was highly theatrical (in the best sense), and for a few minutes the audience enjoyed the spectacle of something approaching big acting. The one piece of comic relief in the play, the Porter's scene—which the austere Coleridge described as " the disgusting passage " that was probably an interpolation of the actor's—came to life in a remarkable way owing to Frank Pettingell's performance as the castle's bibulous butler. *The Times* said : " Drunken Scotsmen do not change with the years," and, as one saw in the production of *The Taming of the Shrew* at the Court a month or two later, Shakespeare's genius for seizing on the comic characteristics of his fellow men would seem to be more adaptable to modern conditions than such tragic figures as Macbeth and Lear, whose motives are definitely fixed by time and place. The murder of Lady Macduff (Chris Castor) and her Eton-collared son had a poignancy that was emphatically heightened by the clothes of to-day, and Macduff's reception of the news of the death of his wife and children made a profound impression on the audience owing to the moving acting of Scott

82

Sunderland, who was dressed in an ordinary lounge suit for this scene. Obviously, it was the military uniform that was the cause of a good deal of the trouble.

But *Macbeth* is a proverbially unlucky play, and every old actor has a dozen stories to tell of the disasters that have followed a production. It is an extraordinary coincidence that everything that could possibly go wrong did so at the Court. The scenery fell down during the first week, and on the day before the opening H. K. Ayliff arrived at the theatre to find that the dress circle was on fire ! It was a Sunday, the fire brigade was called, and by some miraculous means the seats were replaced in time for the first performance.

There was an amusing echo of the production a few weeks later in *The Elizabethan*, the Westminster School Magazine, in which it was recorded that a resolution deploring the representation of Shakespeare in modern dress was defeated in a school debate. It was evident that the boys were all for modernity, for one speaker suggested that Macbeth should wear a cloak the colour of which should be changed by an electrical device to symbolise his varying moods. Another young critic pointed out that the recent production at the Court was no criterion. If Mrs. Siddons and Garrick acted in modern dress, why shouldn't we ? was asked. Yet another pertinent speaker suggested that as Bernard Shaw would sue anybody who produced *Saint Joan* in modern dress, it was " a low dodge to take advantage of the deceased Shakespeare."

CHAPTER XI

A REVIVAL OF "METHUSELAH"—STAGING TENNYSON'S "HAROLD"—
ANOTHER MODERN-DRESS PRODUCTION

THE month's revival of *Back to Methuselah* on March 5, 1928, was
very popular, and it proved that Mr. Shaw, like all great dramatists,
wears well. Four years before, the metabiological pentateuch
occasioned so much cheap ribaldry that G. B. S. had refused to take a call
on the last night, but this time it was noticeable that the appreciation increased
as the play progressed. Instead of being performed on consecutive nights
the five parts were spread over three weeks, one and two occupying the first
week, three and four the second, and the fifth part being given in the third
week. Then the whole cycle was twice performed right through during the
fourth week. St. John Ervine wrote three long notices in the *Observer* in
which enthusiasm was tempered by some acute criticism. In the last article
he said that he had " obtained more pleasure from the performance of this
great play than from anything he had seen or heard in the English theatre for
a considerable time." He was probably right in his assertion that the tre-
mendous power of the play would only be apparent on the day when a continuous performance of the entire piece is given, and he suggested that it would
be an excellent notion to do this on a Sunday. He instanced the production
of the whole of *Brand* in Stockholm in 1885. It began at 6.15 p.m. and
ended at 1.15 a.m., and Mr. Ervine added boastfully that the rest of us also
belong to the Nordic race and are as capable of sitting through a long play as
is any Swede or Norwegian. No doubt Sir Barry will take his advice one
day, for, however the divisions are made, the lack of continuity in *Back to
Methuselah* does dissipate the interest.

It was possibly owing to the fact that Lord Oxford had just died that Mr. Shaw cut out the references to " Mimi " and made some other slight modifications in the character of Lubin in part two. Clifford Marquand again appeared as Lubin, but this time he wore a pointed beard. Edith Evans was free to play the Serpent and the She-Ancient, and most of the members of the original cast at the Court were in the company.

New ground was certainly broken in the next production at the Court when Barry Jackson followed Shakespeare, Shaw, and ultra-modern expressionism by a production of Tennyson's *Harold*, which was published in 1876 and had never been presented on the regular stage. Two years before, however, F. Frankfort Moore had made an " actable version " of the play, which had been performed—curiously under the title of *1066*—at a pageant at St. Leonards-on-Sea. On that occasion it had been cut down to three acts, and the tragedy played for three hours. The sonnet that Tennyson wrote on the site of the battle of Hastings was used as a prologue " by way of reparation," according to Mr. Frankfort Moore, " for liberties taken with the text."

Barry Jackson had intended for some time to stage Tennyson's neglected drama, which Henry Irving considered " quite impossible " for the reason, no doubt, that it did not provide him with a suitable part. The original idea was to put on *Queen Mary*, but both Sir Barry and H. K. Ayliff came to the conclusion that *Harold*, with its lovely lyrical qualities and its stirring scenes, deserved production in London. *Becket*, of course, had run for over a hundred nights at the Lyceum and was twice revived ; *Queen Mary* had also been acted (with less success) by Irving ; Ellen Terry had appeared in *The Cup*, and the Kendals had played in *The Falcon*. The plays were written in the days of the great actor-managers, none of whom apparently saw himself as Harold, and it was left to Barry Jackson (who had spent most of his theatrical career in giving England an idea of what a National Theatre ought to do in this country) to rescue it from the book-shelf.

It is interesting to recall the circumstances under which Tennyson wrote the play. They are related in the son's Life of his father.

" When we were at Battle Abbey in 1876, where my father wrote his prefatory sonnet to *Harold*, we found a rising ground to the English right, and he pictured Edith and Stigand and the English Canons of Waltham and the Camp-followers standing to watch the battle, and to catch a glimpse of their great Harold, between the English standards which flapped high above the roof of flying arrows, and the deadly gleam of axes that lightened with a single flash about the summit. And when we saw the streams of tourists flowing over the lawns, and not seeming to care much for this mighty Harold or for the momentous field of Senlac, he turned to me and said :

> " ' Another England now we come and go,
> A nation's fall has grown a summer's show.' "

Tennyson called the play a *Tragedy of Doom*, and on its publication there were reviews of several columns in most of the newspapers. Longfellow writing from America described it as " a voice out of the Past, sonorous, semi-bar- baric "; Browning said it was " another great work, wise, good, and beauti- ful "; and Aubrey de Vere wrote : " The extreme simplicity of the drama requires a corresponding amount of strength to make it effective, and a sort of Æschylean strength seems to belong to it everywhere."

It cannot be said that the London critics of 1928 were as powerfully im- pressed by the drama on the stage as the Victorian poets were by the play on the printed page. Perhaps over-conscientious, they were prejudiced by a preliminary reading. But E. A. Baughan found that the blank verse—which is " rather mawkish to read "—came out better on the stage than he expected. James Agate thought *Harold* dull. It " is a capital example of the good, competent thing in which it is difficult to find faults or take interest." *The Times* in a very graceful notice can hardly be said to have been enthusiastic : " The narrative never falls into the shadow of monotony. But it never emerges into the full light of poetic imagination. It is not dull; it is, on the contrary, a tale that one is compelled eagerly to follow; but it never takes fire, sweeping the spectator from remembrance of himself." S. R. Littlewood, in the *Morning Post*, was uncompromising in his criticism: "There was no getting away from the sheer tedium of Tennyson in Sir Barry Jackson's production of *Harold*; so much of it is not merely blank verse, but blanket verse, smothering every natural expression with a pall of old convention." Ivor Brown came to the conclusion that nobody except Shakespeare could have made the Saxons interesting on the stage, and Shakespeare did not attempt the task.

In *Harold* several very impressive scenes stand out in the play, which, however distinguished, is not essentially dramatic. Shakespeare faced the full implication of his story and developed his characters on the stage, whereas Tennyson—with the instinct of the poet rather than that of the inherent dramatist—was inclined to burk the issue at important moments. The play is an epic narrative inspired by the poet's genuine concern—in which there is the merest touch of snobbery—at the attitude of the careless crowds at Battle Abbey, and it was particularly appropriate that Gwen Ffrangcon-Davies should open the play in a charming dress of 1876 and speak the "Show Day" prologue. The decorative note was emphasised throughout the play, and Paul Shelving's lovely curtains and costumes are among the major work of this fine artist. The company had for the most part been trained by H. K. Ayliff in Birmingham, a school in which the actors had been given plenty of opportunities for speaking verse, and the actors were not afraid of the Tennysonian cadence or the rich music of the phrase.

One would not say that the casting was ideal, for the part of Harold demanded Martin Harvey, Henry Ainley, and several other romantic actors rolled into one. It was played by Laurence Olivier, who had made a distinguished appearance as Malcolm in the modern-dress *Macbeth*. He was then in the early twenties, and had received his apprenticeship with the

Birmingham Repertory Company on tour after a short training at Miss Fogerty's School. It is interesting to recall that it was Olivier who created the part of Stanhope in the original Stage Society production of *Journey's End*, and would doubtless have played it during the long run if he had not been under contract to Basil Dean to act in *Beau Geste*.

What Olivier lacked in romantic stature he made up for in fire and intensity of speech. It was a remarkable performance for a very young man, for he spoke musically and sincerely; at the same time Harold demanded more weight of personality and a greater experience. Scott Sunderland was brilliantly cast as William, making the Norman Conqueror a figure either debonair or as "stark as death"—according to the scene. George Howe made the most of the death-scene as Edward the Confessor; there was a touch of dry humour in Clifford Marquand's performance as Stigand, and there were particularly good character studies from Robert Speaight and Ralph Richardson. Gwen Ffrangcon-Davies was charming in the shadowy part of Edith, and she sang the delightful song composed by Ernest Irving exquisitely. As nightingales are rare in Sloane Square a gramophone record of a duet between Beatrice Harrison's 'cello and the nightingale in her Surrey garden served as a lovely refrain; in fact, this snatch of music and Paul Shelving's brilliant decorations are the most abiding memories of the production.

It is amusing to recall that the first night of *Harold* clashed with the presentation of *Gentlemen prefer Blondes* at the Prince of Wales's Theatre, and, as "Sir Topaz" (who can now be identified as James Agate) said in a witty article in *Eve*, most of the highbrows preferred the Anita Loos farce on that occasion. Not only did many of the dramatic critics send their "second-strings" to the Tennyson play, but intellectuals like H. G. Wells, Arnold Bennett, and Edward Marsh sat "sunning their noble selves in the smile of Miss Loos's gold-digging heroine." "I asked Mr. Bennett," wrote "Sir Topaz," "why he was not looking on at Tennyson, and for an answer received a smile and a shrug of the shoulders which, however, suggested that in honour of the poet he had sent his carriage to the Court Theatre."

So much for what " Sir Topaz" called the " exhumation of *Harold*" !

The special spring season at the Court ended with the last of the modern-dress productions, *The Taming of the Shrew*, proving itself considerably more amenable to the treatment than *Macbeth*, which H. K. Ayliff himself has admitted was a failure. After the Kingsway *Hamlet* Ayliff accepted an invitation to go to Vienna and do a modern-dress production in that city with Moissi as the Prince of Denmark. It was so successful that offers came to him from Reinhardt in Berlin and from other places abroad, an indication of the amount of interest that was caused by the revolutionary method of staging the plays. He was unable, owing to other engagements, to accept these offers, but after the production of *Yellow Sands* in America the Shuberts suggested that he should stage a modern-dress production of *The Taming of the Shrew* for them in New York with Basil Sydney as Petruchio. It ran at the Garrick Theatre in New York for twenty-two weeks, despite the fact that during the rehearsals the Shuberts lost heart in an enterprise which they thought was foredoomed to failure. Ayliff records that he was not even invited to the opening performance. He actually paid to stand at the back, and had the gratification of seeing the enthusiasm of the audience and hearing his name called at the end.

The London production followed the one in New York very closely, and it was, with one or two exceptions, very favourably received by the critics. *The Taming of the Shrew* is simply a rollicking Elizabethan farce which gains by being treated as prose. It needs to be rattled off at a great pace, whether it is played in ancient or modern costume. One had the feeling at the Court that Shakespeare—who, after all, was a dramatist and not a costume designer—would have enjoyed the fun as much as the audience, which was certainly not the impression left by the Hollywood version of the *Shrew* made by Douglas Fairbanks and Mary Pickford.

The artificiality of the play is heightened by the Induction, which in the earliest version, published anonymously in 1594 (and ascribed to Greene with possible assistance from Marlowe or Shakespeare), ends with Sly on the stage. As R. Crompton Rhodes pointed out in one of his illuminating articles in the *Birmingham Post* this early play was probably " vamped up " from memory by the actors, and in this connection it is of interest to record that Barry Jackson was tempted to use the old ending—with Sly in his own clothes before the inn awakening from the dream which had taught him how to tame his shrewish wife—and actually rehearsed it, but it was eventually omitted owing to the difficulties of the text. In the Folio Sly fades early out of the play, but as Crompton Rhodes said, " comics will be comics," and there is every reason to think that the beggar remained in his place almost to the end.

It is extraordinary that the Induction has been omitted so often, for it provides just the right kind of farcical attitude of mind in the audience. It makes a high-spirited " rag " of what would be intolerable as a serious comedy. At the Court it was treated as a " rag," in which Kit Sly was the victim of an unsporting practical joke by the local Hunt. Played by that superb character actor, Frank Pettingell (who afterwards acted so well in *The Good Companions*), Sly lurched out of the alehouse on the heath—which was almost certainly run by a Trust Company !—before the lord arrived with his musical comedy chorus of huntsmen. After the familiar preliminaries he was placed in a stage box, in which he was addressed from the apron—a convenient concession to the traditionalists erected for the occasion.

The play was performed by the members of the " Birmingham Rep. Company," as the basket carried by the strolling players was labelled. Although the action took place in Padua the characters wore modern English dress with the exception of Grumio, who appeared in some of the later scenes as a black-coated Fascist. It was a charade, and not for a moment was it necessary to believe in the violence of Kate, the forcefulness of Petruchio, or the sweet imbecility of Bianca. But it was all good fun, and the initial tussle between the lovers was especially exciting owing to the spirited acting of Eileen Beldon and the glorious confidence of Scott Sunderland. They took the scenes at a fine galloping pace, and Kate's final capitulation was first-rate comedy. Shakespeare's share in the play was certainly written with his tongue in his cheek, and one was surprised, not only that Miss Beldon delivered the " moral " at the end with such serious intent, but also that the producer left out the final couplet :

Hortensio : " Now go thy ways, thou hast tamed a curst shrow."

Lucentio : " 'Tis a wonder, by your leave, she will be tamed so."

Mercifully we were saved the dreadful wink with which Miss Pickford gave a lie to the whole of the artificial business at the end of the talking film.

H. K. Ayliff set his ingenious mind to work to get as much fun as possible out of the production. The greatest joke of all was to set Act IV, Scene 5, in the manner of the first act of *Doctor Knock.* The scenery moved, and Petruchio's apostrophe, " Come on, i' God's name ! " was addressed to the starting handle of the motor in which the bridal party returned to Padua. At the wedding reception there was of course a press photographer and a cinematograph operator, who recorded the row at the end when Kate felled a bridesmaid with a well-aimed bouquet. Comic business was introduced with the slightest excuse in the text. For instance, Grumio pointed to Gremio's trousers when he retorted, " And that his bags shall prove," and Curtis, asked to produce a fire, brought on an electric stove.

Perhaps the most noticeable thing in all the modern-dress productions has been the stage effectiveness of certain characters who have always seemed swamped in costume. Partly due to Ralph Richardson's delightfully amusing performance, Tranio leapt into life as a Cockney chauffeur who masquerades so perkily as his master. Such fine crisp comedy could only have been achieved in present-day clothes. But the whole team worked together with enjoyable zest, and one recalls with relish Clifford Marquand's portrait of a distinguished old gentleman in Baptista, and Nigel Clarke's easy-mannered Lucentio, and Wallace Evennett might have stepped out of the Palais Royal as Gremio. Muriel Hewitt looked irresistibly arch as Bianca, Edward Chapman gave a distinct and quick-witted study as Grumio, and Drusilla Wills was very amusing as the slightly inebriated housekeeper, Curtis.

Although *The Taming of the Shrew* finished the special programme of five plays at the Court, it was not given up until November 1928, when Sir Barry finally ended his association with a theatre that he had held for nearly four years. There was a four weeks' revival of *The Farmer's Wife*, in which members of the touring company—including Ernest Stidwell as Churdles Ash—appeared. It was followed by the production of Harris Deans' comedy, *Aren't Women Wonderful !*, and finally the *Yellow Sands* touring company filled the bill for a few weeks before the theatre was given up.

Enough has already been written in this book about the two Phillpotts's comedies, and there is very little that need be said of Mr. Deans' play. It had been presented successfully at Birmingham, and Mr. Ayliff made one of the few mistakes of his career when he attempted to elaborate the production for London. The introduction of a song, " Aren't Women Wonderful !"—a catchy little number with words by Desmond Carter and music by Vivien Ellis—was intended to give liveliness to an ordinary domestic comedy, and it had the effect of being entirely out of place in a piece that started brilliantly in the kitchen of a middle-class maisonette and, in any case, fell to pieces when the characters arrived in Kensington. In the first act Mr. Deans proved, as he had done before, that he could write good dialogue. The scene was realistic, and yet not merely photographic, for there was an artist at work placing his characters unerringly in their setting. It was good craftsmanship that promised a delightful play about everyday people. Needless extravagance crept in, however, and the more flamboyant of Ben's relations became a nuisance. But Con Hawley, the wife of the young inventor, and the wonderful woman of the title, was consistently charming, owing to Dorothy Turner's impetuously graceful acting. She was the mainstay of the play, although Ralph Richardson's performance as her husband, Ben Hawley, had just the right touch of ingenuousness. Nevertheless, it was difficult to take very much interest in Ben Hawley's amorous adventures with the seductive wife of the capitalist who was financing his invention. It was no fault of Isabel Thornton that her part of a good-natured musical-comedy actress became irritating, for she played with admirable restraint, and kept the character from lapsing into caricature, and one admired the acting of Clifford Marquand as the financial magnate, and Dorothy Holmes-Gore as his affected wife. It is interesting to recall that Kathleen Harrison was in 1928 acting the type of maidservant that she is still presenting with such devastating insight to-day. It is unfortunate for an actress to be so perfectly right in the creation of a character, for she is doomed to do nothing else for the rest of her career.

CHAPTER XII

" BIRD IN HAND "

DRAMATISTS as well as actors are expected to conform to type, and it is a criticism of the theatre to-day that a note of surprise always heralds a new departure by a playwright or a player. When Barry Jackson staged *Bird in Hand* there were exclamations of astonishment that Mr. Drinkwater, known chiefly as the author of *Abraham Lincoln* and other austere chronicle dramas, should turn his hand to rural comedy. At least the play was usually described as that, and comparisons were drawn with Eden Phillpotts; in reality there was very little resemblance between *Bird in Hand* and *The Farmer's Wife*, and in no sense can it be said that Mr. Drinkwater was taking a leaf out of the Phillpotts's book.

Bird in Hand, originally produced at the Birmingham Repertory Theatre in September 1927, was first seen in London at the Royalty on April 18, 1928. The critics who compared it with *Caste* were nearer the mark than those who dragged in the name of Eden Phillpotts. For Mr. Drinkwater presented the old problem and gave it a modern twist. Thomas Greenleaf comes of a yeoman stock, and his family has kept the Bird in Hand inn in Gloucestershire for a couple of hundred years. He is a Conservative who believes in class distinctions; the Squire is the Squire and always has been, just as the Greenleafs have always been innkeepers—self-respecting, God-fearing—but nevertheless that is the station in life to which they have been called. Unfortunately for his ideas, Thomas Greenleaf sent his only daughter, Joan, to a high school, and her education has made her a fit companion for the Squire's son, Gerald Arnwood. The two have been for motor rides together, and when the innkeeper hears of these innocent " goings on " he is very disturbed in mind. Did not a Greenleaf in the eighteenth century go out for a ride in a gig with one of Gerald's ancestors ? The consequence of that affair has remained the one skeleton in the Greenleaf cupboard. The innkeeper is therefore taking no risks, for he feels only harm can come of this mixing of the classes. It was useless talking to him about modern ideas, for he reckoned that human nature on a summer night in the twentieth century was very much the same as it was two hundred years ago. So he forbad the trip to Cirencester that evening. Joan is a charming girl, but she refuses to be bullied, and defies her old-fashioned father. As luck would have it, there is a violent storm, and the news comes to the inn that the young people are sheltering in a summer-house in the Squire's grounds.

It is very unlikely that Thomas Greenleaf had seen *Our Betters*, but he might have read a criticism of Somerset Maugham's play. Anyhow, he remembered the fate that befell her great-aunt, and concluded that the worst had happened. So, in the middle of the night, the three guests at the inn— Ambrose Godolphin, K.C., Mr. Blanquet, a traveller in sardines, and a bright young spark named Cyril Beverley—hear a rumpus in the adjoining room. Joan's father is threatening to break down her door unless she unlocks it and lets him in.

The visitors intercede at the request of Mrs. Greenleaf, who has been a circus rider and does not share her husband's " diehard " views, and it is decided to try " the case " in the bedroom with the King's Counsel as Judge. The matter is thrashed out as in a Court of Law, Godolphin, in pyjamas, adopts his most forensic manner and the various parties have their say. Greenleaf makes a long, excellently written speech, in which he argues that class is class, and that if the gentry have lost their class consciousness he is determined to keep *his* place.

The old man is soothed into a more reasonable frame of mind, and the case is adjourned until the following morning, when the Squire himself arrives. In order to win Greenleaf's consent, he amusingly suggests that Joan is not

Costume Design for Dame Miolans
in
"The Marvellous History of Saint Bernard"

good enough for his son. The parent is immediately roused in defence of his attractive daughter and all ends happily.

Bird in Hand is a good-humoured and very human play, in which the comedy continually borders on farce without stepping over the edge. In less skilful hands it would have been farcical, but Mr. Drinkwater has founded his theme on the firm basis of character. His people are alive, they have been well observed and dexterously presented. One had the notion that the author, who lived in Gloucestershire for some time, had originally been taken with the idea of embroiling three stray visitors in an old country inn in a domestic quarrel. He succeeded admirably, and differentiated his characters delightfully. His sketch of Mr. Blanquet—French, and not pronounced " Blanket " as he is careful to explain—the Cockney sardine traveller from Balham, is a most charming creation of a man with an eager and sympathetic outlook on life. It was a shame to clothe his humility in a tail coat, straw hat, and brown boots. Such a bait to catch the groundlings was unworthy of the character and the play. Ivor Barnard gave a lovely performance, and in his quiet, wistful sincerity lived down his grotesque clothes. Then there was Felix Aylmer as the lawyer, suave, precise, and amusingly pompous, with Charles Maunsell as the third of the trio. Herbert Lomas has played scores of obstinate parents in his time, and he took Greenleaf in his stride. It was one of his best performances, for he brought out the essential charm and lovable-ness of the man, but he was helped by the author, who presented all the members of the company with " grateful " parts. Jill Esmond Moore, the daughter of famous parents, was graceful and high-spirited (without being pert) as the rebellious daughter; and Amy Veness, Patrick Susands, and Frank Allenby admirably portrayed the other characters.

The play received almost unanimous praise from the Press. *The Times* said: " To laugh with ease and lightness; to hear a plain tale well told; to witness acting which is for the most part full of life and invention—this is to enjoy one's evening in Mr. Drinkwater's company." In the *Observer*

St. John Ervine described *Bird in Hand* as " an exceptionally pleasant comedy," in which the most notable quality " is the essential decency of all its characters."

Ivor Brown was " grateful to Mr. Drinkwater for a comedy which brings an urbane wit to the rural scene, and comes as a nice reaction to style and manners in the midst of so much noisy nonsense." *The Nation*, however, was disgruntled.

" How pleasant," its critic wrote, " it is when journeying across the bitter sandy waste of the twentieth century to come on an undefiled oasis of pure Victorian imbecility, the blissful inhabitants of which never seem to have had one idea in their lives. Such an oasis is the ' Bird in Hand,' a Gloucestershire public-house, which that incorruptible highbrow Mr. John Drinkwater has just erected at the Royalty Theatre. The art of Victorian drama consists in choosing a very serious subject and then in refusing to take it seriously. The result is known as ' wholesome optimism,' and has rather discredited the age of Victoria in the eyes of future generations. If you want to know how the son of the Squire fell in love with the very refined daughter of the innkeeper, how her hot-headed old father, proud of his yeomen quarter-ings, objected, how his wife was sensible, how he had to give way, how a dry old K.C. showed a wise humanity, how a Cockney commercial traveller can be the subtlest of philosophers, and how all is for the best in the best of all Rousseau worlds, go to the Royalty and find out. Personally, I thought *Bird in Hand* almost too silly to be pardonable. But then there is that wise saw, *tous les goûts sont respectables*, which unfortunately human beings insist on treating merely as a cloak for their own depravity, rather than as the starting-point for a really liberal state of mind."

Hubert Griffith, in the *Evening Standard*, had a somewhat similar objection to what he called " a silly and nauseously sentimental little play." " By all means," he said, " let us have a study of the interesting problem of someone

98

'marrying beneath them,' as the phrase goes, but let us have some of the normal and elementary considerations dragged in!"

These last two reviews are quoted because they are examples of the bad kind of criticism which objects to a comedy because it is not something else. The suggestion is that Mr. Drinkwater, as a stern artist, should have faced the subject realistically, and discovered some of the grimmer implications of a marriage between rich and poor. As well object to Shakespeare's bright-hearted treatment of Sir Toby Belch and Sir Andrew Aguecheek. The first should obviously have been the subject of a dramatic exposure of the evils of drinking and Sir Andrew is certainly a case for the doctor! It is, of course, stupid to labour the point.

Bird in Hand ran for nearly a year. It was actually withdrawn on March 2, 1929; it was kept going by Barry Jackson because he believed in it, but the play lost money in London. The American production was exceedingly successful. It ran for about a year in New York and afterwards on tour; and probably created a record for an English domestic comedy in America.

The Mayor, which is dealt with in the chapter on the Phillpotts's comedies, followed *Bird in Hand* at the Royalty, and after that the theatre was given up.

CHAPTER XIII

THE Arts Theatre Club, with its own comfortable and tastefully decorated theatre and a membership which ensures that an experimental play will have an audience for a short run, serves several useful functions. One is that it has on several occasions provided the Lord Chamberlain with the opportunity of seeing a play that he has banned from being acted on the public stage. It is an opportunity of which he is always glad to avail himself, and in many cases he has reversed his judgment and issued a licence for ordinary performance. The most notable instance was *Young Woodley*; another was *Six Characters in Search of an Author*, which Barry Jackson staged at the Arts Theatre on May 20, 1928.

It was *Six Characters in Search of an Author* that first introduced an English audience to Pirandello, for the play was performed by the Stage Society in a translation by A. A. Greene at the Kingsway on February 26, 1922, with Franklyn Dyall as the father, and Muriel Pratt and William Armstrong as the stepdaughter and her half-brother. That, of course, was a private performance for the members of the Society. But the play was allowed to be acted publicly in the original language by the Italian company which visited the New Oxford Theatre three years later, surely an illogical action on the part of the Censor who had refused to license the English version.

The English rights of *Six Characters in Search of an Author* had been acquired by Barry Jackson in 1923 for production at the Birmingham Repertory Theatre, and the Arts Theatre gave him a chance of staging the play for the first time, and thus getting the ban removed. The earlier version was discarded, and H. K. Ayliff was responsible for the new adaptation which is now the authorised one for production in this country. It was used by Anmer Hall at the Cambridge Festival Theatre, and again last year when the play was revived at the Westminster.

Described as "a comedy in the making," the play is probably the finest of Pirandello's; or, at any rate, the best that has been seen in England. It is at once a brilliant satire and a parable of the mind of the artist. What is truth? What is reality? Pirandello asks; and his answer is to bring on to the stage the six characters who have been discarded by the dramatist because they have refused to follow the direction of the plot. They insist on working out their own destiny. This fantastic theme is the familiar problem of the creative artist. Bernard Shaw has admitted that his characters have a way of taking charge of their own careers, and St. John Ervine once confessed that an author "may even be compelled to change his intention . . . and find himself, after sitting down to write a tragedy, obliged to rise up having written a comedy. The wind bloweth where it listeth: so do ideas."

As Crompton Rhodes pointed out in his article on *The Six Characters*, even Falstaff would not obey Shakespeare. "If you be not cloyed with fat meat, our humble author will continue the story, with Sir John in it, and make you merry, with fair Katherine of France, where, for anything I know, Falstaff shall die of a sweat!" Thus he promised at the end of *Henry IV*, but old John refused to go again on the stage—he fumbled with the sheet, and played with flowers like a child, and babbled of green fields, and so he went out at the turning o' the tide. Who can doubt that he died in this way, and that Shakespeare cried at his death-bed, as one who had lost his dearest friend?

Is the idea so fantastic after all? Hamlet, Mr. Pickwick, Sherlock Holmes . . . they have an existence that is not the less real because they never lived. Pirandello himself was obsessed with these six characters who stood by him "in the shadows, and in the silence he could hear their

102

very breathing" . . . and the play was his method of getting rid of the obsession.

But it is a mistake to insist on the philosophic background of Pirandello's plays at the expense of their dramatic content, or to take them as seriously as a textbook on metaphysics. The Italian author has a very moving story to tell in *The Six Characters*, and not the least part of the pleasure at the theatre is to see it emerging from the chaos of unexpected characters who crowd the empty stage, all of whom find their places in the magnificent pattern. It is similar to the thrill experienced in watching *Warning Shadows*, one of the first German silent films to discard captions. In his production at the Arts Theatre H. K. Ayliff did not attempt to preserve the Italian atmosphere, and he made a point of differentiating between the "characters" and the theatre company. The father in the Italian company had red hair, which matched his violent persuasiveness, whereas Walter Pearce made the character thoroughly English, playing him, as Mr. Rhodes suggested, as a part that was being lived rather than acted. By contrast, D. A. Clarke-Smith and Dorothy Holmes-Gore, as the leading man and leading woman, were actors, and they succeeded admirably in exhibiting the affectations and the humour in the stage people. Dorothy Black, according to *The Times*, gave a "vivid performance as the stepdaughter, in which impudence, hungry passion, and frenzied vindictiveness are clothed in a curious disturbing beauty," and the meeting of the father and the stepdaughter—the episode which was the chief reason why the play was originally banned in English—was described by the same critic as a "tragedy that bears its grim verisimilitude in every line" and "haunts the imagination with redoubled power in this revival." Fewlass Llewellyn as the producer, Margaret Chatwin as the mother, Isabel Thornton as the infamous dressmaker, Colin Keith-Johnston as the son, and the other members of the company gave excellent support.

The play was produced at the Arts Theatre on May 20 for four performances, at which there were crowded audiences. It attracted so much interest that Barry Jackson arranged with Sir Alfred Butt to transfer it with the same cast to the Globe on May 28. There was a heat wave at the time. The cheaper parts of the house were full, and there were indications that a stalls and dress-circle audience (without which it is of course impossible to run a play) would have been attracted, but Barry Jackson was abroad, and the Globe management had stipulated to work to a weekly figure that was never reached. The play was therefore withdrawn at the end of a fortnight.

Altogether Barry Jackson has staged three plays at the Arts Theatre, the other two being *The Shadows of Strife* on December 9, 1929, and *Demos— King and Slave* on July 1, 1931. John Davison, the author of *The Shadows of Strife*, is a young mechanic in the locomotive sheds at Mexborough, and the play was his first successful literary venture. It was awarded the annual prize offered by the Sheffield Playgoers, and performed by these enterprising amateurs several times, afterwards being staged at Leeds before it was acquired for production at the Birmingham Repertory Theatre. The author, who is now in his early thirties, had been writing since he left school at the age of fourteen to become a fitter's apprentice, but none of his stories had been accepted. A journalist had told him that he had a gift for dialogue, and during the General Strike he started *The Shadows of Strife*, which is a dramatisation of the experiences of the men and women in a Yorkshire mining village during and after that great industrial upheaval. It was completed in three months. The author, with only his weekly wages to keep a wife and several children, could not afford to get the play typed for the Playgoers' Competition. Nevertheless, it was accepted immediately, and with the small royalties that he received from the performances he paid for typed copies to be sent to managers. Fortunately one fell into the hands of Barry Jackson, who arranged for the production of the play at Birmingham on October 19, 1929. Two months later he gave the author an opportunity for his play to be seen in London, and Cedric Hardwicke joined the Birmingham Company for the two performances. He was then appearing in *The Apple Cart*, and it is a proof of his

104

keenness that he snatched what leisure he could, and hurried to Birmingham for rehearsals. He took the part of the grandfather who had been crippled by a mining accident years before. It was, in Mr. Ivor Brown's opinion, " a performance of extreme beauty. The blend of pinched and pallid age with a full and bloodshot theology to be seen in the old Bible-reading cripple was a masterly piece of North-country portraiture, and Mr. Hardwicke cut it out in rock with a masterly hand. "

The strength in *The Shadows of Strife* is its fine, sincere, well-observed characterisation; and its weakness, the melodramatic element that found its way into the plot. The members of the family were humanly drawn, by a man who knew the people at first hand, and had the instinctive dramatist's gift for making them effective on the stage. The mother, with her long-suffering air, her courage and fatalistic resignation (so well depicted by Cicely Oates); the shrewd modern daughter (acted by Daphne Heard), and the two sons (played by Norman Claridge and Kenneth Frazer) being particularly interesting studies. Altogether *The Shadows of Strife* revealed in Mr. Davison a dramatist of great promise. He has written at least two other good plays, *Sair Jane and the Seekers*, which certainly deserves to be seen at some time, and another, about the Brontës, that has been acquired by Barry Jackson.

If *Demos—King and Slave* had been produced before *The Apple Cart* it might have created a deeper impression. It is a satire on democratic govern-ment, and Ghéon seemed rather clumsy after the witty wisdom of Bernard Shaw. Curiously enough, Barry Jackson's version, with lyrics by John Drinkwater, produced at the Arts Theatre on July 1, was the first performance of the play in any country, although it had been written several years before. It is un-necessary to dwell at length on this essay in the Aristophanic manner, for it is not likely to be heard of again. Barry Jackson staged the play out of loyalty and friendship to Henri Ghéon, with whom he had been so delightfully associated in *The Marvellous History of Saint Bernard*. It was a difficult piece to produce, for the author is satirising modern political institutions with his

105

characters in a Greek setting. Both speech and costume blended the past and present, but it was generally felt that the humour was laboured and the Royalist notions were trite after the Shaw play. Andrew Leigh's ordinariness as Demos was too near to life to be effective on the stage, and the best performances were given by Walter Hudd, who represented monarchy in Themistocles with upstanding youth and sincerity, and Agnes Lauchlin, the Political Muse who had the best lines in the play.

During the spring season at the Court in 1928 there were some special performances of *The Third Finger*, a comedy by R. R. Whittaker, a Yorkshire journalist, at that tiny home of big endeavours, the Everyman at Hampstead. The play had been originally produced at the Leeds Arts Theatre in November 1925, and the fortnight's run in London followed immediately upon the revival at the Birmingham Repertory Theatre where it had been deservedly very popular. In better circumstances more might have been heard of Mr. Whittaker's amusing little piece, which was based on a novel idea and had its share of witty lines. Perhaps the tale wore a trifle thin at times; but nevertheless the author made good entertainment out of the charming heroine's revolt against spinsterhood, typified in the wedding-ring that was unlawfully worn on the third finger.

The ring had, of course, magic properties. Not that a magician appeared when it was touched, but the possession of it transformed the scholastic-looking spinster of twenty-five into a radiant young beauty with shingled hair and lovely clothes. But it also entailed the necessity of finding a husband—the mysterious Mr. Smith whom she was supposed to have married during a summer holiday—and Mr. Whittaker made admirable use of the farcical possibilities of his theme, before he rounded off the play happily by real wedding-bells.

The Third Finger improved as it went on, and the last act was a good deal better than the first. It was delightfully acted, especially by Melville Cooper. He impersonated the young novelist who started the ball of fun rolling—

and eventually married the girl—with so much zest and such keen and spontaneous humour that the play moved on its theatrical way with delightful hilarity. Lila Maravan looked charming as Marion Stannard, and there were good performances from Isabel Thornton and Maud Gill, as the confirmed spinster-sisters, and the other members of the Birmingham Company.

Every manager knows that a play which is hailed as a big success in Birmingham, or Manchester, or Edinburgh, often falls flat when it is acted in London. Geography counts a good deal more than people think. To "try-out" a piece in the provinces is helpful, because it enables the company to settle down and the producer to adjust minor faults, but it is no certain criterion for London, any more than London is a sure guide for Liverpool or Newcastle unless the play is of a first-rate quality with a universal appeal. In several cases Barry Jackson brought to London plays that had been immensely popular at the Repertory Theatre, strengthened the casts, and the verdict was entirely reversed. One instance was *The White Assegai*, by Allan King, which was first presented in Birmingham on February 9, 1929, and staged at the Playhouse on January 21, 1930. According to the *Birmingham Post*, the impression in the Midland city was that the author had written "a stirring play," and the writer—R. Crompton Rhodes—found "it difficult to say why the play as a whole was less effective at the Playhouse."

Godfrey Tearle was engaged to take the part of Hardress MacKenzie, the beloved Commissioner for the M'soi territory in South Africa, who is the central character in a play that promised to be of a much better brand than the average type of drama which features a strong silent hero in one of the outposts of the Empire. It opened well. One believed in MacKenzie, the sympathetic ruler whose word was law to the natives. He was the third of a noble line of administrators, for father had handed down to son the tradition of justice. The M'Soi may have had other gods, but their chief object of worship was MacKenzie. Unfortunately there was a Mrs. Hardress MacKenzie whose heart was in the South-western postal district or at Ascot, and certainly not in that particular sun-baked portion of Africa which Paul Shelving depicted so picturesquely in his settings.

The problem of the first act is repeated in the second, where the newly arrived bride of the local station-master is found pining as ardently for her native suburbia as the Commissioner's wife longs for Berkeley Square or Hurlingham. But the author found it necessary to illustrate his thesis (that station-masters and commissioners would do their jobs more efficiently if they left their wives at home) by a dash of melodrama, and the audience became less interested in the play after the white assegai was thrown. Godfrey Tearle was splendidly in his element as Hardress MacKenzie; and of the other performances those of Phyllis Shand, who made a perfect little study of the station-master's wife, Daphne Heard, Harry Wilcoxon, Norman Claridge, and William Heilbronn stood out most vividly.

One of the critics ended his notice of the play—which had only a short run at the Playhouse—being followed, on February 13, 1930, by *Devonshire Cream*—with the statement: "This is the sort of thing that makes the Dominion so cross with us." The author was born in Zululand, and had practised as a barrister in South Africa. He replied:

"In fairness to the management and the producer of the play, if not to me, I should like to point out that the High Commissioner for the Union of South Africa was present at the first performance of this play, and was good enough to express to me afterwards his appreciation of the angle from which the play was written, its treatment, and its fidelity to facts, so far as this is desirable or capable of achievement in the theatre.

"Furthermore, other South Africans present on the same occasion have expressed similar views."

To which the critic replied, "As a South African born and bred I claim the same right to express an opinion as other South Africans present."

108

CHAPTER XIV

" THE APPLE CART "

A T the end of 1928 Barry Jackson was feeling disheartened about his efforts in the theatre, as he confessed to Bernard Shaw in the letter which is quoted in the first chapter. G. B. S. not only gave his advice, but offered him his next play. In addition he became a very active partner in the Malvern Festival, an enterprise of far-reaching importance, which will probably be regarded by theatre historians as one of the most valuable achievements of our time. The full story cannot be told in this book, which is limited to Barry Jackson's London work, but in the last three years Malvern has been so closely allied to London that it continually comes into the picture. It is doubtful if, without the inspiration of Malvern, Barry Jackson would have continued in management. But he threw himself with great zest into the festival. It was the fulfilment of an idea that he had cherished for many years, and *The Apple Cart* came at an opportune moment, as it brought about a turning-point in his career.

In the autumn of 1929 Barry Jackson ceased for a time, anyhow, from being what might be called an experimental manager, putting on plays in small theatres for short runs, and he took over the Queen's in Shaftesbury Avenue, at first on sharing terms with Sir Alfred Butt and the following year as tenant. The change in policy was due largely to the advice of Cyril Phillips, the general manager for all Barry Jackson's enterprises, who is that rare combination—a first-rate business man and a person of judgment and taste. Years before, Mr. Phillips had insisted on being engaged in some capacity at Birmingham, and he actually started as a sort of superior office-boy to Bache Matthews. When the company came to London he had charge of most of the arrangements, and it is safe to say that Barry Jackson would have lost a good deal more money than he did if it had not been for the guiding hand of his young assistant. Cyril Phillips was able to persuade Barry Jackson to go into a bigger theatre, and the change to the Queen's was the beginning of something like prosperity. It meant that the big shop window in the heart of the West End of London helped to pay for the Birmingham Repertory Theatre, the Malvern Festival, the Canadian tours, and other such luxuries.

The record from the production of *The Apple Cart* in September 1929 until the early part of 1932 has been excellent, for Mr. Shaw's play ran until May 24, 1930. The Queen's was again taken over from September on lease from Maurice Browne (who had by that time acquired it), and *The Barretts of Wimpole Street* was played to enormous houses until it was withdrawn on January 2, 1932. Then followed the short revivals of *The Farmer's Wife*, and on April 5 the first production in this country of the ill-fated *Caravan*, which will be dealt with in a later chapter. There is nothing more irksome to Barry Jackson than long runs, but he has realised that if he is to keep going at all he must accept the position. What he would like to institute in London is the repertory system, adopted in most of the State and municipal theatres abroad, where such pieces as *The Apple Cart* and *The Barretts of Wimpole Street* would be kept in the bill for years instead of having their popularity exhausted in long runs. There are obvious difficulties in the way, but it is pretty certain that if such a pioneer effort is ever started in our time Barry Jackson will have a hand in it.

One important thing that should be realised is that the experimental seasons at the Court and the Kingsway had their share in training playgoers to appreciate something other than the purely frivolous in the theatre. *The Apple Cart* and *The Barretts of Wimpole Street* would no doubt have been successful under any circumstance, but possibly these plays would have had shorter runs if the ground had not been prepared by Barry Jackson and one or two other managers who were not afraid of putting on intelligent plays.

Almost everything that it is possible to say about Bernard Shaw has already been said, but there is one quality of his that should be mentioned—his faculty for recognising the right manager and sticking to him. When Barry Jackson ventured on *Back to Methuselah* G. B. S. offered him the first refusal of *The Apple Cart*; and the Theatre Guild of New York was given the refusal of his plays for the same reason.

It is noteworthy that none of Mr. Shaw's later plays has been produced first in this country. The explanation according to Mr. Shaw is not, on the whole, creditable to the British Press. In 1913 the German managers, in despair at having to produce his plays after they had all been reported from London as unpleasant failures, stipulated that in future the first performances should take place in Germany. Accordingly, *Pygmalion* reached the stage in Berlin before its famous production by Tree at His Majesty's Theatre; and since then it has been Mr. Shaw's practice to give priority to foreign theatres whenever possible. The Guild staged *Saint Joan*, *Back to Methuselah*, and *Too True to be Good* before they were done here; and G. B. S. gave permission to his Polish translator, Floryan Sobienowsky, for *The Apple Cart* to be presented by Dr. Szyfman at the Teatr Polski in Warsaw before it was seen at Malvern. The success of *Saint Joan* had made a Shaw *première* an event of world importance, and on Friday, June 14, the dramatic centre of interest was shifted to Warsaw where, in the finely conducted Polish Theatre, *Wielke Kram*—a title conveying almost exactly the same meaning as *The Apple Cart*— was presented to an audience that included the President of the Polish Republic. The fact that *The Times*, the *Observer*, and the *New York Times* sent special correspondents and printed long criticisms indicates the importance that was attached to the opening.

It is doubtful whether any play received such an extraordinary amount of attention as *The Apple Cart*, for the newspaper articles that followed the production at Malvern would fill two or three huge volumes. A disadvantage of the Warsaw opening was that one or two critics arrived at their conclusions before seeing the play. Hannen Swaffer, for instance, wrote several columns before and after Malvern, and in a preliminary article he described the play as " ponderous and dull." That was in the *Sunday Express*, and in the American *Variety* he said that " it merely sounds like a lot of drivel " which " might thrill the inhabitants of Choctaw, Mich., but, frankly, I do not think it is worth while going three hours in a train to see."

But Mr. Swaffer went, and with him some seventy or eighty journalists, in the special train on Sunday, August 18, 1929, to be present at the *répétition générale* of *The Apple Cart*, which was to open the Malvern Festival on the following day. The occasion was unique in the English theatre, and it was unfortunate that the " critic's express " arrived very late and so delayed the start. The play was acted before a large and distinguished audience, for in addition to the journalists, a number of managers and other important people in the world of art and letters were present. It is safe to say that there is no other dramatist who could have shifted the focus of attention to a small town in the West of England on a Sunday afternoon in the middle of summer. The first English performance of *The Apple Cart* was an event of international importance, and it set the seal of success on the Malvern Festival for that season and future years.

Mr. Shaw sat in the front row of the dress circle—the seat he has continued to occupy at all the festival performances. But he vanished with the cheering at the end and Barry Jackson was left to acknowledge the applause. On the previous afternoon, however, there was some excellent speech-making in the public library at Malvern on the occasion of the opening of the Bernard Shaw Exhibition, which contained the Rodin bust, an Augustus John portrait, photographs of scenes of the plays taken in many countries, and some of Paul Shelving's designs. The ceremony was performed by Sir Edward Elgar, who paid a delightfully amusing tribute to Mr. Shaw. In his reply Mr. Shaw said :

" It is a curious thing to be standing talking in the middle of an exhibition when that exhibition is almost myself. The gratifying part of the thing to me is that the exhibition has been opened by Sir Edward Elgar. I would say one word in defence of literary men. Shakespeare, who really in a way had to compose his own, was all right on the subject of music. That could be seen not only by his direct references to music, but also by the pleasure he had in making fun of it. In *Much Ado About Nothing* Shakespeare got a great deal of fun out of music in a way that no man who was not a lover of music could possibly do.

"We are advancing. My friend H. G. Wells is a really remarkable performer on the pianola. My friend Arnold Bennett gets as far as performing pianoforte duets, at least one half of them. We really are not so Philistine as we used to be. Of course, if you compare my career—it would flatter me very much—with that of Sir Edward Elgar, you will see that I had a very easy job in comparison with his. I don't think any of you, except perhaps those as old as myself—which must be a small percentage of this or any other audience—can form any conception of what the British theatre was when I started.

" It had got down to the pitch of having absolutely no ideas, and, further-more, having a distinct theory that the theatre must not have any ideas. You were not allowed to talk about love affairs, not allowed to deal with that subject really, but only to skirt round it in a kind of way. If you had a heroine, her marriage was put off by improbable events of one kind or another, until it was time for people to go home.

" As a matter of fact I had a clean slate to begin on. If you read my first play you will probably think it is an execrable one, hardly fit to be performed at the present time. But I can assure you that it was discussed in the whole of the London press for a fortnight. It was an extraordinary thing. Everybody agreed that I could not write a play at all, and had completely shown my ineptitude for the theatre. It has been perfectly easy for me to become a distinguished playwright.

" Compare that with Sir Edward Elgar's start. He had to come in on top of Beethoven and Wagner. The difference is enormous, but he succeeded in doing it; he got away with it. He has been alluded to to-day as the greatest English composer. When I was a young man, if you said anybody was the greatest English composer the reply was H'm-m. That was not saying much. As a matter of fact Sir Edward is one of the greatest composers of the world. If you make the utmost allowance for the very greatest of his contemporaries you must say that he is one of the four best composers in the world. If you asked me to name the other three I could name one or two pretty quickly, but when I came to the third I should be very much puzzled.

"That is something for England to be proud of. But I do not think England is proud; that is the disgraceful thing about it. But the fact remains that in comparison with Sir Edward Elgar—although I am rather a conceited man, and in comparison with any other artist in England feel that I can carry my head high—I am sincerely and genuinely humble in his presence. I re-cognise a greater art than mine and a greater man than I can ever hope to be.

"I just want to say one little word about the exhibition. Several young ladies will be asking puzzling questions about it, for instance, why so many of the men are in modern dress whereas all the ladies are in fancy dress. But they are not. In my time women used to dress like that. You saw them about in the streets in that sort of costume.

"I have one advantage, in that I come here not to celebrate what I have done myself by myself. You will see by these photographs a large body of artists, and it is their work which has made my work live. There are people who can read a musical score in such a way that Sir Edward Elgar can put his music before them and, though it is not possible to hear it, the music exists for them. That is not my case. My play does not exist until we have a body of artists. You have a distinguished body of artists here in Malvern who have done a lot of wonderful work, and some of the things they will do in the course of the Festival will astonish you. They have astonished me. A great deal that is going to be done is going to be very wonderful as a mere artistic feat. I get the credit."

114

Mr. Shaw had some spirited things to say about the destruction of the Malvern Hills by quarrying, and suggested that the great gashes should be filled up with old theatre tickets; but he only made one important reply to the critics of *The Apple Cart*, and that was given to the present writer in a long interview in the *Observer*. For, although the play had an enthusiastic reception from the audience at the special matinée, the "Press" was decidedly mixed. It was G. B. S. in a new mood, and the admirers of *Saint Joan* were frankly disappointed by the farcical elements in this serious discussion on democratic government. Here are extracts from some of the notices:

The Times critic found the Interlude in the second act "so dull and pointless that it is hard to imagine what persuaded Mr. Shaw to write it." For the rest of the play "is prophecy sharpened by satire, backed by reason and, though damaged now and then by buffoonery, undistorted by prejudice. . . . Except in rhetorical fragments it is not Mr. Shaw at his full range, but the first and last acts, taken together, are good entertainment, and make up a pamphlet on democracy which may silence many a catchword and charm away many a pious delusion."

W. A. Darlington in the *Daily Telegraph* said: "*The Apple Cart* is not one of Mr. Shaw's best plays, but it is packed full of interest. It shows very clearly once more, what was shown in *Back to Methuselah*, that Mr. Shaw is a firm believer in the aristocratic principle—that is, that the success of any system of government depends not on the system, but on the men who administer it."

Ivor Brown in *The Manchester Guardian* said: "Mr. Shaw has cast himself, in the opinion of any democrat, as the devil's disciple," and he expressed the fairly general feeling that "on the whole it is Mr. Hardwicke's occasion, and it is to the actor rather than the author that Malvern will bring added laurels."

Hubert Griffith in *The Evening Standard* came to the conclusion that *The Apple Cart* was the work of "a new and unknown young dramatist, a Mr. G. Bernard Shaw," who must be fifty years the junior of his famous namesake. "I guess him as a young man of twenty or thereabout, of extraordinary power, promise, and erratic achievement, a sense of humour alternatively penetrating the juvenile, and a recklessness as regards dramatic presentability common to every young man just down from the university with his first play in his pocket."

Hannen Swaffer wrote that the new play " exposes " Bernard Shaw " as a man behind the times. At the age of seventy-three he has nothing new to say," and at the end of his long notice in the *Daily Express* added that he went to Malvern to see a great play. He had forgotten that weeks before he had said that he had expected " drivel."

The *Daily Herald* had a long, reasonable article by R. S. Pippett, who said: " It is often exciting and often stimulating (the man couldn't write an un-interesting play), but to what end ? . . . Where are you running to, my merry master ? " . . .

It was Mr. Shaw's old friend and fellow-campaigner, H. W. Nevinson, who came out in the *New Leader* with the fiercest criticism of a play which he said was " badly constructed in its dramatic form and pernicious in its moral." He contrasted " the tall slim figure of nearly fifty years ago who like myself was hanging on to the skirts of literature and journalism " with the hero of the " smug prosperity of Malvern," and after a long—almost heartbroken—examina-tion of the plot, said that " all the tyrants of Europe will delight in the play."

Mr. St. John Ervine anticipated Mr. Shaw, and answered some of the more blatant of the critics in the article he wrote for the *Observer* :

" Any person who asserts that *The Apple Cart* bored him publishes his own shame : he acknowledges that he is fit only to sell beetroot. The intellec-tually-bankrupt and the spiritually-damned will yawn their fat heads off while this piece is being performed, but that precisely is what we would wish them to do.

" Fat heads ought to be off ! It will be sufficient, perhaps, for the discern-ing if I say that a thousand persons drawn from every part of these islands, and including visitors from foreign countries, of whom less than a hundred were what may be called professional playgoers, witnessed the performance with interest and delight.

" *The Apple Cart*, which is as disconnected as a revue, is not, of course, a play, but who cares whether it is or not ?   Mr. Shaw spent a long life in writing plays which are not plays, and has persuaded people all over the world to prefer them to plays which are plays.   It opens with a discourse on ritualism which has as much relevance to the rest of the play as the old-fashioned overture had to the rest of the opera.

" This discourse is added to the play in exactly the same spirit in which the gargoyles were added to cathedrals, out of sheer exuberance and overflow of genius.   The second act is almost an independent piece, and might, with little alteration, be performed by itself.   The end is more or less in the air. But what an entertainment !

" To produce such a piece of high farce, fantastic wisdom, and brilliant discourse at the age of seventy-three is a feat of which men half the age of Mr. Shaw might be envious, and I feel impatient with the paltry yammerers who complain that its author is out of touch with life.   What life ?   Whose Life ?"

The interview in the *Observer* appeared three weeks after the original production, and was given by Mr. Shaw in a talk at Malvern, at which Cedric Hardwicke was present.   As G. B. S. explains in some detail the political significance of *The Apple Cart*, the article is reproduced more or less as it appeared in the paper :

" Critics rely very much on labels," Mr. Shaw said.   " I was not shown a proof of the programme, and therefore the sub-title, which will be printed when the play is seen in London, was omitted.   The full title should have read : *The Apple Cart—A Political Extravaganza in Two Acts and an Interlude.* The word ' extravaganza ' would have helped them, and they might then have been less worried by the short second act.

" Although it is an ' extravaganza ' the play has a serious background ?

117

" So serious that I intend to tell Mr. MacDonald when he returns from Geneva that he must refuse to take any young man into his Cabinet who hasn't seen *The Apple Cart* at least six times. It is intended as a salutary lesson, as I feel it is a state of things into which we could drift.

" Few of the critics have realised that one of the points of the play is the recognition that there is no governing class. By which I mean the real governors are not a class, but are members of all classes. The King sees at once that Boanerges, who was picked out of the gutter by a policeman, is of the governing class. The revelation that comes to Boanerges is that the King is also a member of the governing class. The ' plain man ' joke between the King and Boanerges has upset one or two people, but as a matter of fact it is a piece of tactful diplomacy on the part of the king. ' I'm a plain man,' boasts Boanerges. ' Not at all,' protests the King—the usual joke, it is asserted —but the King, after a pause, adds, ' You are anything but plain ; in fact to me, you have always been an enigma.'

" Curiously, too, the Prime Minister has been called a dummy and a fool. But Proteus is really a very elaborate study of an able man. The King represents the classical example of the governing type ; Proteus the womanly type—' I use the word woman,' added Mr. Shaw to his wife, ' in the stage sense.' He is hysterical and gets flustered, but he jumps at the true position of things at once, as I show at the end of the play, when he immediately grasps the fact that the King has beaten him. In the first act, too, Proteus and the King, in the two minutes they have together, arrive at a complete understanding. More is accomplished in that time than in the half an hour's previous talk.

" But the main oversight in the criticism of *The Apple Cart*," Mr. Shaw said, " is the failure to grasp the significance of the fact that the King wins, not *qua* King, but *qua* potential Commoner. The tearing up of the ultimatum is almost a defeat for him. It is certainly a defeat for Lysistrata (The Power Mistress), whose depression the King shares when the shouting is over.

" The critics have also missed the point of Boanerges's refusal to listen to a word against the Democracy which he himself ridiculed as an instrument of popular government. The Strong Man is a democrat because Democracy places power within his reach. As Magnus expressly says, Democracy has destroyed responsible government and gives the power to (as Bunyan put it) ' Him that can get it.' ' Yourself, sir, for instance ? ' says Lysistrata. ' I think I am in the running,' replies the King. But the great point is that he thinks he is in the running as Able Man, not as monarch. Only once in the whole play does Magnus assume royal authority, and that is in the Interlude when he cries, ' Orinthia, I command you.' And then both Orinthia and the audience laugh him to scorn.

" No serious student of how monarchy and democracy actually work will demur to my handling of them," Mr. Shaw added. " The protests that have actually been made sound as if George Odger had risen from his grave !

" Now, about the second act—the Interlude ? "

" Composers are permitted a slow second movement in their symphony ; why shouldn't I be allowed one in my composition ? " Mr. Shaw protested. " Or, if you prefer it, the second act is a piece of relief, comic relief, if you like. What has the grave-diggers' scene to do with the character of Hamlet ? But Shakespeare understood what I understand—if you put humour into a play it must be cheap humour !

" The second act has, of course, a great dramatic significance, as great a significance as the porter's scene in *Macbeth*. It completes the portrait of the King who in the middle of the crisis is seen, not merely as a statesman, but as a human being with a domestic life."

Here Mr. Hardwicke suggested that the King held the Cabinet in the third act with some of Orinthia's powder still on his uniform.

" Symbolically, yes," Mr. Shaw said, " nevertheless, Hardwicke, I hope that you will always brush your coat before the third act. The King knows that in married life the important thing is the recognition of the other's limitations.

There are some subjects he cannot talk about to Jemima, his wife, and, on the other hand, the beautiful Orinthia certainly has *her* limitations. It is an important scene, and not there merely to amuse. I can only conclude that the critics who did not understand it are happily married to wives who combine in themselves Orinthia and Jemima. The average man is not so fortunate. There are hundreds of nice middle-class families who do not understand why they squabble. The scene between the King and Orinthia will serve as a dose of castor oil. Shakespeare suggested the same idea when Beatrice says, in reply to Don Pedro's proposal, ' No, my lord, unless I might have another for working days ; your grace is too costly to wear every day.' Jemima, intellectually, is good for everyday wear, and Magnus knows this ; Orinthia is the splendid Sunday relaxation. Married people will get on better after they have seen the second act of *The Apple Cart*."

The Apple Cart was brought to London on September 17, 1929, after a fortnight's season at the Birmingham Repertory Theatre, and there was a brilliant audience at the first night. Mr. Ramsay MacDonald may or may not have read Mr. Shaw's remarks in the interview, but he was there and talked to the author before the curtain rose. Among the others present were H. G. Wells, Arnold Bennett, Lady Astor, Prince Bismarck, and Sir Ernest Wild ; and the Prince of Wales visited the play during the course of the run. The critics who went again were more favourably impressed—Mr. Darlington, for instance, found that repetition sharpened the appreciation—and James Agate and E. A. Baughan, who saw the play for the first time, wrote very appreciative notices : Mr. Agate said that Mr. Shaw " is the greatest mind which has done honour to the English theatre in the last three hundred years," and Mr. Baughan described *The Apple Cart* as " one of the most brilliant plays Mr. Shaw has given us."

There was universal praise for H. K. Ayliff's production and the acting by one of the finest teams ever brought together on the stage. Most of the players were familiar members of Barry Jackson's company, and they were used to acting together; they were in fact a team, with Cedric Hardwicke carrying his bat brilliantly through an innings that lasted three hours. He was certainly "not-out" at the end, and during the first week at Malvern took such parts as Shotover, Cæsar, and the "He-Ancient" in his stride. His King Magnus is one of the greatest performances of our time; quiet, sincere, exquisitely poised, sympathetic, and always—even in the extravagant inter-lude—perfectly dignified. Those who found little to admire in the play had nothing but praise for Mr. Hardwicke. By the time *The Apple Cart* reached London the actor had settled down comfortably into the part, and the slight suggestion of nervousness that was evident at the opening of the play at Malvern had disappeared. He seemed intellectually in tune with the author's concep-tion and the collaboration was perfect. The long speech on the working of democracy was beautifully "timed" and delivered with smooth distinction, and throughout the play his intelligence, humour, and gentle irony gave life and reality to Mr. Shaw's lines.

Ivor Brown said in the *Manchester Guardian*, "Edith Evans brought the glamour of a Congreve part to the hard radiance of Orinthia." Charles Carson admirably expressed the touch of authority behind the wily, senti-mental, and hysterical Prime Minister, and the Cabinet was excellently por-trayed by Matthew Boulton, as the noisy and clear-thinking Boanerges, Clifford Marquand, Julian d'Albie, Aubrey Mallalieu and Frank Moore, and Dorothy Holmes-Gore and Eileen Beldon as the two women members. Then, too, there was James Carew's perfect little sketch in the last act of the American Ambassador, and the opening discourse on ritual was enlivened by the acting of Scott Sunderland and Wallace Evennett. G. B. S. admitted in an interview that he had made a "false start." He said that he intended to have two opposing parties—the Quakers and the Ritualists—but found that he could only use the King and the Cabinet. "But," he went on, "I decided to use the false start—the opening conversation between the two secretaries—

as a sort of Mozart overture to the play. I agree, however, that the play would lose nothing vital if it were taken away." It was omitted in the appalling but lucrative travesty of the play perpetrated by Reinhardt in Berlin.

Mr. Shaw had occasion soon after *The Apple Cart* was produced in London to elucidate the report of a conversation he had with a prominent Polish journalist which had been sent out by Reuter and published in several papers.

"I seem to have conveyed to my distinguished foreign visitor," he said, "that the Prime Minister discussed *The Apple Cart* with me after the performance, and that I intended to base King Magnus on the personality of Marshal Pilsudski, but refrained lest it should be said that the Marshal had paid me to do so.

"I also seem to have conveyed that the play has not been received here with the enthusiasm it evoked in Poland. This is not precisely what I meant to say.

"I have not spoken to the Prime Minister since he was present on the first night, when we exchanged a few words before the rise of the curtain.

"I cannot claim the privilege of personal acquaintance with Marshal Pilsudski. I never dreamt of using him or any other living person as a model, though every living ruler in the world will find a melancholy resemblance between his predicament and that of King Magnus.

"I cannot avoid the suggestion that I have been paid by him, because it has already been made, and will probably be repeated *mutatis mutandis* in every country where the play is produced.

"Finally, as to the alleged more enthusiastic reception of *The Apple Cart* in Poland than in London, all I can say is that the reception in London has reached its box-office limit, and that the Polish enthusiasm, however frenzied, can go no farther from the author's point of view.

"Naturally I am glad to learn that King Magnus's crown fits the heads of all the rulers, and that his subjects in all lands vie with one another in appreciation of my picture of their political situation. That is all I need say at present."

122

CHAPTER XV

" THE BARRETTS OF WIMPOLE STREET "

THE second Malvern Festival was again a " slight tribute to the genius of a great living dramatist," and the Shaw programme included *The Admirable Bashville, Candida, Widowers' Houses, Heartbreak House, The Dark Lady of the Sonnets, The Apple Cart*, and *Getting Married*. A new play had been expected, but Mr. Shaw was busy on the Collected Edition of his works and it did not materialise. Some time before, however, Barry Jackson had acquired *The Barretts of Wimpole Street*, by Rudolf Besier, and it was a felicitous idea to present the play in the first instance at Malvern. For it was at Hope End, near Ledbury, six miles away, that Elizabeth Barrett spent the happiest days of her youth. " The Malvern Hills," she wrote years later, " seem to me my native hills, for though I was born in the County of Durham, I was an infant when I went first into their neighbourhood, and lived there until I passed twenty by several years." There are many references to the district in her poetry. Much of the time she spent out of doors, and it was in the fields at Hope End that she fell and injured her spine when she was saddling her black pony Moses. This accident was the beginning of the long illness that lasted until Robert Browning carried her off to Italy as his wife. The family left Hope End in 1832 when she was twenty-six, and three years later settled in No. 50 Wimpole Street, where Elizabeth Barrett spent so many years as an invalid " in the darkened upper chamber of a cheerless house "—the scene of Mr. Besier's play. It was not until May 20, 1845, that Robert Browning entered that austere household and sixteen months elapsed before they

" . . . sloped to Italy at last
And youth, by green degrees."

123

Ledbury is proud of its associations with the poetess, and in the Barrett Browning Institute in the village there are complete sets of the works of Elizabeth Barrett Browning and Robert Browning, as well as many old letters and records of the family.

The Barretts of Wimpole Street was produced at Malvern at the matinée, on Wednesday, August 21, 1930. It was a thrilling experience to be present at the first performance of a play that has had one of the longest runs in recent years—both here and in America. The readers of the Browning letters may have had some slight fears. How easy it would be to sentimentalise the meeting between Elizabeth Barrett and the impulsive young poet who, before he met her, had written " I . . . love these books with all my heart—and I love you too." That was the thought in the minds of those who had imagined the introduction to the greatest romance in modern history—which was, as Dilys Powell put it felicitously in the *Sunday Times*, the " challenge of truth to fiction." Any such doubts were soon dispelled, for Mr. Besier's dialogue, besides skilfully incorporating many letters and other records, was equal to the superb occasion; and one settled down to a complete enjoyment of a chronicle that was not the less exciting because the events were well known.

Before the meeting of the lovers there was the picture in the first scene of the Barrett household, Elizabeth on her couch being prayed-over by the dominating father, Edward Moulton-Barrett, the high-spirited Henrietta making a show of resistance while the others are huddled like a flock of sheep in the corner.

At once the atmosphere of the grim house in Wimpole Street was established. As Ivor Brown said, " The air was as heavily charged with fear and gloom as that of Dotheboys Hall." Against this background, so finely realised by the author and the producer, H. K. Ayliff, the love story stood out in crystal clearness, the beauty being heightened by its setting. The critic of *The Times* talked of " the shock of surprise and delight with which Mr. Besier's study of the Brownings comes to the audience." It was the same writer who, after again praising "the courage and the grave beauty of its approach to the main theme," pointed out what he considered a "serious fault" in the play: "Mr. Barrett is drawn as a man tormented by a profound and insane sensuality. He drops into an ugly flirtation with his own niece, but wrests himself from it in time. Later, while pleading for his daughter's affection, he is betrayed into what is, and what Elizabeth perceives to be, an incestuous impulse."

Other critics also had references to the author's presentation of the character of Mr. Barrett: "terrible psychological portrait"; "disagreeable and disconcerting element"; "a Cenci, an unnatural creature with incestuous impulses," were some of the phrases, and after consultations with Mr. Besier, it was decided to modify the scene between Mr. Barrett and his pretty niece, Bella Hedley, and the final episode between the father and daughter. When the play reached London on September 23, the papers welcomed the slight alterations which were mainly of production. Very little in the text was altered, but anything that might be construed as offensive was toned down in the playing of the scenes.

In an article in an American journal Mr. Besier said: "I had lifted him (Mr. Barrett) bodily out of the best biographies of the Brownings, the memoirs of his contemporaries and the letters of his devoted daughter, Elizabeth, extenuating nothing, nor setting down aught in malice, and I had done what I could to account psychologically for his aberrations, his tyrannies, his perversities, and his cruelty."

The Times notice, however, had the effect of making public the private quarrel between the author of The Barretts of Wimpole Street and the grandchildren of Edward Moulton-Barrett. It had begun some time before, following a newspaper paragraph announcing the play which indiscreetly referred to Mr. Barrett as "that ogre parent of the Victorian age." The present head of the family thereupon wrote to Mr. Besier demanding a manuscript of the play for consideration. This was declined, and letters came from other members of the family, and finally from lawyers stating that it must not be produced without their full approval. Fortunately the Lord Chamberlain is the arbiter in these matters and he had passed the play subject to certain alterations and cuts in some of the passages which concerned the character of Mr. Barrett.

The Barretts of Wimpole Street opened on August 20, and nine days later the following letter appeared in *The Times*:

"To the Editor of *The Times*.

"Sir,—

"In a review of the play, *The Barretts of Wimpole Street*, published in your issue of August 21, it is stated that 'Mr. Barrett is drawn as a man tormented by a profound and insane sensuality'; that 'he drops into an ugly flirtation with his own niece'; and that 'while pleading for his daughter's affection, he is betrayed . . . into an incestuous impulse.' On these amazing representations your reviewer somewhat strangely comments: 'Whether there is or is not biographical evidence in support of this need not immediately trouble us.' 'Mr. Besier is writing a play, not a biography, and may at a distance of eighty-five years claim imaginative licence.'

"Permit us, sir, to inform your reviewer that there are at this moment alive 12 grandsons and granddaughters of Mr. Barrett, all of whom cherish in their memories the strong affection and respect with which to the end of their days he was regarded by his sons and daughters, including the poetess herself and her sister Henrietta. The production of this play has already caused them much pain, knowing how deeply it would have been resented by the whole of the persons depicted in it. But they were totally unaware of this charge of 'insane sensuality' and 'incestuous impulse' which your reviewer exposes.

"We desire, therefore, as emphatically and plainly as possible, to state that there is not a stiver of biographical evidence or evidence of any kind to support this vile suggestion, and that it is totally inconsistent with the whole

126

character and life of the man libelled. To bring so disgusting a charge against a dead man without any foundation can only be deemed a monstrous abuse of the dramatic art and a gross violation of the canons of literary decency.

"It is a misfortune that the law provides no remedy against the gravest and most despicable libels on the dead; but surely if it is permissible for a dramatist to endeavour to attract spectators to his plays by enduing characters in them with unspeakable vices, he should be compelled to utilise only imaginary persons for that purpose, and should be restrained from defiling with his filthy imaginings the reputation of real men, whose memories are still dear to the living.

"We write this protest as some of the grandsons of Mr. Barrett, and are, sir,

> Yours very truly,
> E. A. ALTHAM, *Lieut.-General, R.P.*
> H. P. MOULTON-BARRETT, *Lieut.-Colonel, R.P.*
> E. M. MOULTON-BARRETT, *Lieut.-Colonel, R.P.*"

There is no need to comment on this extraordinary outburst, for Bernard Shaw, who had been present at several rehearsals, and had attended the first performance of the play, stepped into the controversy, and wrote the following letter to *The Times*:

"THE BARRETTS OF WIMPOLE STREET"

"TO THE EDITOR OF *The Times*.

"SIR,—

"There seems to be a good deal of the sultry West Indian temperament left in the Barrett family if we may judge from the letter in your columns in which three of the twelve surviving grandchildren of Mrs. Browning's father accuse Mr. Rudolf Besier of 'endeavouring to attract spectators to his play by enduing characters in it with unspeakable vices' and 'defiling with his filthy imaginings the reputation of real men.' On the face of it the signatures of this startling explosion of tropical fury are chips of the old block. It might have been written by the old man himself, and would confirm the truth of Mr. Besier's drawing if there were not already overwhelming evidence to support it.

"It is clear, from the distinguished rank attained by the three, that they have not suffered socially from the unfortunate circumstance that one of their grandparents was a detestable domestic tyrant who, having by good luck a famous poetess daughter who was beloved and married by a great English poet of the finest personal character, made himself infamous by doing his utmost to separate and make them miserable in a transport of snobbery and jealousy. No dramatic poet could ignore the fact that modern psychology has made very short work of the pretension of such jealousy to be pure paternal piety : all that can be said to extenuate it now is that its victims were formerly able to disguise its real nature from themselves by a maniacal self/righteousness nourished by ecstasies of presumptuous and blasphemous prayer. This has been done with masterly art by Mr. Besier, who, in his effort to make old Barrett's personality bearable on the stage, has suppressed the slaveowner's snobbery altogether, and represented him as a being naturally distressed in the two quite delicately treated moments in which he betrays himself to himself and to his daughter.

" If these moments were omitted the tyrant would be left so utterly without excuse, so senselessly malignant and contemptible, that his descendants might plausibly contend that such a monster could not possibly have existed.

"Not even a triumvirate of a general and two colonels should court/martial a playwright without seeing his play, nor should they even during a heat wave of Jamaican intensity use madly intemperate language. Mr. Besier has let down the Barrett family very easily indeed. He has made all the brothers and sisters of Elizabeth so amiable that the audiences that revelled in the play at Malvern will be at a loss to imagine how such blameless ladies and gentlemen

Design for Act Drop
in
" Cæsar and Cleopatra "

could have transmitted so much of their father's arbitrary temper to their three military children.

"Yours truly,

GREAT MALVERN, *August 29, 1930.*   "G. BERNARD SHAW."

This letter was returned to Mr. Shaw a day or two later, as the Editor declined to publish it.

It so happened that the writer was staying with Barry Jackson at Malvern when the letter to *The Times* came back, and suggested to Mr. Shaw that the weekly newspaper on which he was then employed should have an opportunity of printing this protest. Mr. Shaw agreed, and the same day sent the original *Times* letter and the following covering statement:

" On August 29 *The Times* published an extraordinary letter from three members of the Barrett family charging Mr. Rudolf Besier and Sir Barry Jackson with the worst misdemeanour a theatre manager and author can commit: one compared to which card-sharping or cowardice in the field by a military officer, or the secret maintenance of several supplementary husbands by an archbishop's wife, is venial and pardonable: namely, the exploitation of vice—and unnatural vice at that—on the stage to attract money to the box office. The Lord Chamberlain, having guaranteed the propriety of their proceedings, was tacitly implicated in the charge, with the difference that, whereas the alleged motive of the author and manager was greed of gain, Lord Cromer could have no apparent motive except a perfectly disinterested love of devilment for its own sake.

" Now *The Thunderer* is a great newspaper; but at long and rare intervals it goes politically mad; and every August it goes grouse shooting, and leaves the paper to continue with its own momentum. As there is no political convulsion now occurring, and as grouse shooting is in progress, I assumed that the grouse were responsible for the insertion of the letter. But it never occurred to me that *The Times*, having (carelessly, I think) inserted such an abominable accusation, could not foresee that an answer was inevitable, and must be accorded the same publicity. Judge of my amazement when, having carefully watched three performances of the play on which the charge was based, and addressed a letter to *The Times* on the subject, it was returned to me with a courteous private note to say that its insertion would break a rule against discussion of new plays which had been relaxed in favour of the Barrett family only in consideration of their relationship to the characters depicted. The rule is a very expedient one; but its strict enforcement in-volves the exclusion of all imputation of base motives to the persons responsible for the plays. If *The Times* publishes a heated statement that a well-known author, a leading manager, and the chief officer of the King's household are, in effect, corrupt depravers of public morals, no office rule can absolve it from the obligation to give equal publicity to at least a mild suggestion that it is not these three gentlemen who have lost their characters but their three accusers who have lost their tempers.

"As a matter of fact, Lord Cromer generously exceeded his official obligations in considering the susceptibilities of the Barrett family; and Sir Barry Jackson and Mr. Besier met him half-way in this exercise of private good feeling. But they could not, in the face of history and psychology, go to the length of representing Robert Browning as a common fellow who took advantage of a lady of good family, Elizabeth Barrett, as an abandoned female and ungrateful daughter whom no respectable parent could pardon, and her father as a suffering saint of unimpeachable social position for whose untimely decease Britannia still mourns. And it is, I think, plain that nothing less would satisfy their accusers.

"I append a copy of the letter I addressed to *The Times* without further comment, except that as I do not think the acting editor read the Barrett letter as carefully as I did, I forgive him."

Again the Editor declined to enter into the controversy, especially as the statement criticised the attitude of another paper, and Mr. Shaw's spirited defence of Mr. Besier's play is here given in full. Mr. Shaw handed the letters to Barry Jackson, and he has given permission for their publication in this book. It is doubtful if G. B. S. would have been able to convince the older members of the Moulton-Barrett family, who made a further attack in the newspapers on the morning of the London production.

" To the Editor of *The Morning Post.*

" Sir,—

" From reading the criticism of the provincial production of Mr. Rudolf Besier's play, *The Barretts of Wimpole Street* (to be produced at the Queen's Theatre to-night), I gather that it introduces to the public my grandfather as a most disgusting and offensive personality.

" I do not know on what evidence the author can have based his horrible idea.

" Unfortunately the law (I understand) permits one to attack the character of the dead.

" There is no evidence of any sort that my grandfather could be truthfully described as he has been, and I protest most emphatically against a part which every decent man or woman in the country must feel ashamed to face.

" How could such a suggestion be made, when Mrs. Barrett Browning wrote constantly to her father, even to the last ?

" Mr. Edward Moulton-Barrett was a man beloved and respected by his family.   " H. P. Moulton-Barrett.

" (Lieut.-Colonel, R.P.)."

One thing remains to be said about what has been described as the " Besier-Barrett battle." Although the grandsons vigorously opposed the play and refused to go to a performance, the great-grandchildren and the great-great-grandchildren went to see it, and two of them, with stage ambitions, actually applied for parts in the touring company !

The Barretts of Wimpole Street ran until January 2, 1932, it was a great success from the beginning, and in the fifteen months the gross receipts totalled well over £100,000. It was a triumph for author, producer, and actors. The company remained practically unchanged throughout the long run, although Cedric Hardwicke left the cast for a few days in August 1931 in order to appear at the Malvern Festival in *The Switchback*. It was generally agreed that his performance as Mr. Barrett was one of his finest portraits; it presented, in Ivor Brown's words, "a fresh phase of his power, being an essay in vibrant domination and feverish malaise"; Mr. Hardwicke dominated the play as the stern, implacable father dominated the members of the family. There was strength and austerity and a power that was almost terrifying in his acting. It brought into relief the lovely calm, sensitive beauty of Gwen Ffrangcon-Davies's performance as Elizabeth. This actress is never less than very good, and many of her performances have been appraised in this book. It was the general opinion that the poetess in *The Barretts of Wimpole Street* was her best work, and it would certainly be possible to say that it is difficult to imagine the part being better played, for the soul of Elizabeth Barrett, with her fineness of spirit and her glorious courage, came alive on the stage. In the meeting between Robert Browning, acted with extraordinary vitality and impetuous eagerness by Scott Sunderland, there was all the romance of the letters. Most of the parts were brilliantly taken, and remembered with pleasure are Marjorie Mars's rebellious Henrietta, Susan Richmond's picture of the patient, forbearing Arabella, Eileen Beldon's charmingly sympathetic maidservant, Joan Barry's study of a Victorian minx, and the performances of Barry K. Barnes, Oliver Johnstone, Harry Wilcoxon, Wilfred Caithness (who played Dr. Ford Waterlow and took over Cedric Hardwicke's part on the few occasions that he was absent from the cast) and Aubrey Mallalieu. "Flush" behaved perfectly throughout the run, and never barked at that critical moment in the last scene. The canine actor—Tuppeny of Ware—was changed several times during the run, and when he was not on the stage shared Miss Ffrangcon-Davies's dressing-room with her own engaging black pug.

CHAPTER XVI

"A TRIP TO SCARBOROUGH"—TWO REVIVALS—
"HEARTBREAK HOUSE"—"EVENSONG"

ALTHOUGH Mr. Shaw had finished his new play, *Too True to be Good*, it was not ready in time for the 1931 Malvern Festival, which took the form of a survey of English drama from the early sixteenth century to the present day. The plays presented were *Hick Scorner*, a morality, written about 1513, that had probably not been seen on the stage for three hundred years; *Ralph Roister Doister*; Thomas Heywood's *A Woman Killed With Kindness*; Etherege's comedy, *She Would if She Could*; Sheridan's *A Trip to Scarborough*; Lord Lytton's *Money*; and finally *The Switchback*, by James Bridie, the author of *The Anatomist* and *Tobias and the Angel*. As *The Barretts of Wimpole Street* was still running at the Queen's, a new company was engaged for Malvern. It included, however, Cedric Hardwicke, who was released each Saturday to appear as the doctor in *The Switchback*.

Instead of the modern play, Sir Barry decided to bring to London *A Trip to Scarborough*. The revival was highly successful at Malvern, where the audience admired especially Paul Shelving's lovely decorative curtains and Ernest Thesiger's delightfully affected Lord Foppington; but at the St. James's, where it was presented on September 14, 1931, the play was such a failure financially that it was withdrawn at the end of the first week. Some of Vanbrugh's original dialogue from *The Relapse* (from which Sheridan quite shamelessly lifted *A Trip to Scarborough*) had been restored, and several of the critics enquired why the original had not been produced. On the whole, the notices were favourable, and Ernest Thesiger's performance—which was an epitome of all the stylish grace and empty-headed elegance of the eighteenth century—was enthusiastically praised.

Meanwhile *The Barretts of Wimpole Street* continued at the Queen's until January 2, 1932. Sir Barry then decided to satisfy the popular demand for a revival of *The Immortal Hour*. But in order to give Gwen Ffrangcon-Davies a rest—she had been acting Elizabeth Barrett since August 1930—*The Farmer's Wife* was again put on for a limited run of a month with Cedric Hardwicke in his original part of Churdles Ash. With him were many members of the Court Theatre company, and it was good to renew acquaintance with Melville Cooper's farmer; Evelyn Hope's charmingly gracious Araminta Dench; Phyllis Shand and Eileen Beldon, as the Sweetland girls; Margaret Chatwin's Louisa Windeatt, Isabel Thornton's buxom postmistress, and Maud Gill's Thirza Tapper. Mr. Hardwicke's portrait of the rural philosopher was by now an old master, and its gnarled outline, its deep rich humanity and dry caustic humour came as a surprise to theatre-goers who had only seen the actor in *The Barretts of Wimpole Street* and *The Apple Cart*. The part stood out as one of the genuine stage creations of our time and again one realised how much author and producer owed to Mr. Hardwicke.

The Farmer's Wife kept the Queen's filled with enthusiastic audiences until *The Immortal Hour* was ready for its fourth revival in London on February 9. Although it was staged for a limited run, new scenery and costumes were provided. Ernest Irving, for long an enthusiastic admirer of Rutland Boughton's music-drama, conducted the carefully chosen orchestra and chorus, and it was the general opinion on the opening night that the performance was better than the original London production. Many people who were present had seen the opera a great number of times, for probably no piece in recent history—not excepting *The Beggar's Opera*—has created such devoted admirers. In the audience were Lady Londonderry, who has been to every revival, Lady Cunard, Sir E. Denison Ross and Lady Ross, Lord Castlereagh, and Lady Chaplin; and afterwards Lady Londonderry gave a supper party at Londonderry House, which included the composer, Barry Jackson, and several members of the company.

The Times, in the course of a long notice, said that it was a "worthy revival of a work which holds its place through its distinctive character and the high sense of beauty that pervades the music from first to last." It was a delightful experience to see and hear Gwen Ffrangcon-Davies once more as Etain, and other members of the original cast were Arthur Cranmer as Dalua, W. Johnstone Douglas as Eochaidh, and Dorothy D'Orsay as the Spirit Voice and Maive. Bruce Flegg was the new Midir, and he sang the popular fairy song with insinuating charm.

After two and a half successful years at the Queen's Theatre Barry Jackson then struck a bad patch and staged a play that lasted only five nights. Some time before he had acquired the English rights of Carl Zuckmayer's famous circus drama *Katherina Knie*, which is one of the most popular pieces of the modern German theatre. As Cicely Hamilton has an extensive knowledge not only of German but of Germany the adaptation of the play into English was given to her. It is possibly part of the explanation of the complete failure that she kept too closely to the original and retained most of the Teutonic rhetoric and verbosity. There seems to be no doubt that German plays need very thorough revision for England, and *Caravan* was lacking in dramatic vitality on the first night. Curiously enough, it went so well at the dress rehearsal that one of the directors of the Theatrical Guild of New York, who was in London, was anxious to secure an option of the American rights. As he was leaving for the Continent before the opening performance, he cabled his views to his fellow directors.

It is proverbial in the theatre that circus plays are unlucky. Certainly everything possible happened to *Caravan*. To begin with, H. K. Ayliff was unwell and needed a rest, and the play was not given the best of chances, for the producers were unused to the company. After it was presented in Edinburgh for a trial week Marjorie Mars had to resign the chief part of

135

Katherina, and Eileen Beldon stepped into her shoes. This meant a post-ponement in London, and Ayliff then came in and conducted a week of intensive rehearsals and the play was pulled together.

But the postponement and the change in the cast had set people talking, and the first-night audience came to the theatre expecting a dull evening. Or so it seemed. Anyhow the blight spread to the stage, and the sparkle and freshness and vitality that were apparent at the dress rehearsal vanished, and before the third scene it was more than evident that *Caravan* was a failure.

Scenically, Carl Zuckmayer was given every chance, for Dame Laura Knight and Barry Jackson designed a delightful south German setting and some charming costumes for the circus folk. The effects were excellent, and there was a thrilling moment when the old rope-walker was suspended on the wire above the tent, but it was then too late to save the play. Generally speaking, the actors were a trifle too polite. They lacked the flamboyance and roughness of the small-town circus characters they were supposed to represent, and even Cedric Hardwicke was too conscious of his dignity as the old man. It was a very difficult part, however, and even the best actors are entitled to a failure now and then. This was one of the few times that Mr. Hardwicke was less than first-rate. Maisie Gay had some amusing moments as Bibbo, O. B. Clarence gave a sympathetic portrait as an old clown, and there was a refreshing study of a familiar German type from Wilfred Lawson. The acting, however, was too deliberate, and strangely enough the pace at the first performance was considerably slower than at the rehearsals.

More than once Barry Jackson had provisionally announced his intention of reviving *Heartbreak House* in London, but something had occurred to prevent the plan being carried out. Mr. Shaw's " fantasia on English themes in the Russian manner " was first produced by James B. Fagan at the Court in 1921, it was played at the Birmingham Repertory Theatre two years later, and the play was included in the first Malvern Festival with Cedric Hardwicke as Captain Shotover (the part he took originally at Birmingham). The failure of *Caravan* provided the opportunity for a short revival, and it enabled London playgoers to see Cedric Hardwicke in one of his best parts, a creation of author and actor that has the quality of a Blake drawing.

Again the audience and most of the critics asked what it was all about. "Perhaps," said the *New Leader* in one of the most intelligent of the notices, "it is just a queer criss-cross like life itself, the pattern always eluding us, though sometimes we may get momentary glimpses of it. Most probably, like music and all great art, its meaning is within itself. How, after all, can a symphony be 'explained' save in its own terms?" As the same paper suggested, *Heartbreak House* is so "shot with a strange wild beauty that the two lovely lines of Shelley in the play seemed in perfect company."

It was generally forgotten that when G. B. S. began this study of "cultured leisured Europe before the war" not a shot had been fired, and there were obvious reasons why the play was not produced until 1919. It reveals the author, as probably no other work of his has done, in the rôle of seer—a prophet with a sense of humour—and it is surprising that this was not more clearly recognised. *Heartbreak House* was logically the forerunner of *The Apple Cart* and *Too True to be Good*, written by a man who had stood on "Pisgah Heights" and in Browning's words seen "all of it." Most of the critics confessed that they did not know what it was all about, but without an exception the first act was praised. "It has form as well as substance," said *The Times*, "its humour and its argument, instead of being to each other as a showman's rattle might be to his oratory, are felt to be necessary and inter-dependent parts of the same composition." Others saw only the humour, and as many felt that it was a mistake to keep in the Zeppelin bomb at the end of the play, it seems to suggest that to a number of people the play was little more than a long, drawn-out joke in which there were some brilliantly witty passages.

Fortunately Edith Evans was free for the part of Lady Utterword which she played at the original production twelve years before. This fine actress always excels in characters that are more than a trifle larger than life—in Shakespeare, in Congreve and in Shaw—and what the *Week-End Review* described as her suave insolence was a superb foil to the " prophetic rage " of Cedric Hardwicke as Shotover. Admirable, too, were Leon Quatermaine as the decorative philanderer Hector Hushabye, O. B. Clarence as the gentle Mazzini Dunn, and Wilfred Lawson's sketch of Mangan, the simple business man who was really so complex.

It was difficult to decide upon the play that was to follow the short revival of *Heartbreak House*, for, although *Too True to be Good* was destined for the Queen's, arrangements had long before been made to produce it first at Malvern. It was the beginning of June, Barry Jackson had two or three other plays in hand, but he could not make up his mind which to do. There were difficulties of casting, because Cedric Hardwicke and other people in the company were already fixed for the Shaw play.

While he was facing a dilemma which might have meant that the theatre would have to be closed until September, along came Beverley Nichols and Edward Knoblock's *Evensong*. Edith Evans was acting in *Heartbreak House*, and immediately it was realised that Irela was a glorious part for her. Barry Jackson was in Manchester (where the Canadian Company gave a special season) when *Evensong* was received by his General Manager, Cyril Phillips, who read it at once, saw its possibilities, and caught the next train to the north of England. Within a few hours the decision was made to produce it, and less than a month later—on June 30—the play was presented at the Queen's.

It was a wonderful " first night," and success seemed to be in the air from the beginning. In the intervals the pundits coupled, unashamedly, Edith Evans's name with Bernhardt's, and next morning the critics agreed that she had given one of the biggest performances of our time. Perhaps the finest tribute came a week later from Sydney W. Carroll. In the *Daily Telegraph* he said that Miss Evans by " her consummate artistry and brilliant characterisation proved once more that the modern actress can (if only given the opportunity) prove as dramatically striking, as notable in style and polish, as full of intelligence and capacity for natural truthful portraiture, as any of those long-cherished idols of the past. . . ." Mr. Carroll admitted the opportunity, but many of the critics were grudging in their appreciation of the author's share in the success.

It is a popular thing to say that a fine actor or actress could bring tears or laughter by a recital of the multiplication table—but it is a phrase that means less than nothing at all, for no actor can save a bad play. Nor does it detract from Miss Evans's performance to say that Beverley Nichols and Edward Knoblock had provided her with a part in which—to quote W. A. Darlington —she could " score a magnificent success."

The play was based on Beverley Nichols's novel of the same name which was published early in 1931. Edward Knoblock, who has been called the adapter-in-chief to the English stage, saw a play in the book and suggested a collaboration. They started at once and the work was finished ten days later. The chief character was ready-made, of course, but it was another thing to make Irela—the famous *prima donna* at the end of her career—effective on the stage. In other words, it was not necessary that one should have read the book in order to appreciate the play. The story was to some extent refashioned and one or two new characters were introduced. It would be superfluous to give any detailed account of the plot, for there seems every likelihood that the play will be running when this book is published.

The chief character was identified with Melba, but both authors stated in an interview that they went to some pains to avoid the suggestion that Irela was intended for any individual. It was assumed that the record used in the play was one of Melba's, whereas it was from Puccini's *Manon*, in which she never sang. Beverley Nichols, of course, knew Melba intimately—although, in reply to the statement that he acted as her private secretary, he said, " I am incapable of being anybody's secretary "—and he assisted in the writing of her autobiography; but both authors maintained that the character is an imaginative portrait of any great temperamental genius whose faculties are waning.

At the rehearsals Miss Evans, in expressing her gratitude for the oppor-

139

tunity, said, " Irela is a part in which an actress can swim." About her performance James Agate wrote in the *Sunday Times* of " her magnificent bravura. She walks the stage like a Juno, and when, diadem'd and splendorous, she makes entry at her rival's party, her cloak of blue velvet has the majesty of offended heavens." Here are some of the other opinions :

The Times : " Miss Evans's performance is masterly. Free of affectation, brilliant in its attack, rich in ironic sympathy, it is the making of the evening. There is a moment near the end when Irela, her battle lost, weeps as though her heart would break. Miss Evans weeps very quietly, and the breaking of hearts—an absolute finality—is in her tears."

Philip Page in the " Evening Standard" : " Miss Evans's art is exquisite. When for Diva's reasons tantrums have to be shown, there is no hint of over-doing them. The vitality of the woman, the strange mixture of generosity and stinginess, the humour, the vulgarity, the pluck, and the pathos—all are there."

Ivor Brown in the " Observer" : " Miss Evans plays it straight and hard, never exploiting the antics of a *prima donna*, but presenting, with a wonderful accumulation of fine and merciless shades, the vanity, greed, and devouring egotism of the creature who pouts and preens herself on the summit of fame."

Herbert Farjeon in the " Sunday Pictorial" : " How Sarah Bernhardt would have done that ! And how Edith Evans does it ! Here is a marvellous performance, rounded, complete, and beautiful."

The play was beautifully produced by Athole Stewart and, while it was Miss Evans's night, there was first-rate support from the big company. Violet Vanbrugh was content to bring superb distinction to a small part, Frederick Leister gave charm and interest to the sketch of the Archduke, and there was the brilliant study of Irela's youthful rival from Ethel Glendinning. As admirable were the performances by Joan Harben, Harry Wilcoxon, Beatrix Fielden-Kaye, and the portraits of the manager and the impresario cleverly touched in by Wilfred Lawson and Reginald Tate.

CHAPTER XVII

"TOO TRUE TO BE GOOD"—"FOR SERVICES RENDERED"

WHILE many of the critics thought *Too True to be Good* only a torrent of talk, most of them considered that it would be a success in London. When it is remembered that *The Apple Cart* had an almost equally poor reception by the Press the prognostication seemed justified. The early withdrawal of the play shows how unsafe it is to indulge in prophecy in the theatre.

At Malvern *Too True to be Good* was presented at the first performance in the worst possible atmosphere. The curtain was due to rise at two o'clock on Saturday, August 6, and it actually went up about forty minutes late, and then those of the London critics who were being brought down in the special aeroplane had not arrived. They came in during the first act, some of them rather seedy after the flight against a head-wind.

In spite of the delay and the fact that the dress rehearsal had taken place eight days before, the play went very smoothly. There was an interesting audience, and seats for the matinée and the Saturday evening performance were at a premium. Indeed, one journalist stated in print that he was offered £20 for his ticket by "a wild-eyed lady" who had been unable to buy a seat, a statement that sounds too good to be true !

After the Malvern Festival performances, *Too True to be Good* was taken to the Birmingham Repertory Theatre, where it was acted to packed houses of enthusiastic audiences for three weeks. It had been arranged to present the play at the New Theatre in London, and the "first night" on September 13 was a brilliant function, with G. B. S. as the presiding genius in a box with Mrs. Shaw and Siegfried Trebitsch, his German translator. The production

141

had been heightened and improved, although there were still one or two weak passages, especially in the last act.

Generally speaking, it was well acted; although Cedric Hardwicke had a more difficult task than King Magnus in *The Apple Cart*, he nevertheless spoke Mr. Shaw's sermons magnificently. There were big opportunities for two young actresses, Leonora Corbett and Ellen Pollock, both of whom acquitted themselves excellently; and Ralph Richardson, Walter Hudd, and Scott Sunderland put in some good work.

For the first two or three weeks the business was fairly good, and then the box-office takings began to fall off; it was an expensive play to run, and Barry Jackson decided to withdraw it on October 22, after six weeks in London. The withdrawal came as a surprise to many people, including the author, who blamed the stalls public for lack of support. On November 8 he made a statement in *Everyman*, in response to the Editor's request, answering the question: "Why *Too True to be Good* failed ?" The reply was a plea for a National Theatre:

"You may remember," Mr. Shaw wrote, "that after the old experiment made by Vedrenne and Barker at the Court Theatre in 1904, which was finally pushed as far as it would go, and ended a bit further, Granville-Barker came to the conclusion that he could make a West-End London theatre, playing Shakespeare and highbrow repertory, pay its way if it were rent free and rate free. An endowment to that extent would solve the money problem.

"In those days, remember, rents and salaries and production expenses were so much lower than at present that George Alexander, running the most expensive theatre of its size in London, complained to me that he could not carry on unless his receipts were £1,000 a week.

"Now it happens that this is the exact figure at which *Too True* was withdrawn last Saturday. Alexander would have run the play for six months

142

at such business; but Barry Jackson has to throw in his hand unless the receipts are £1,600.

"When Cochran gallantly produced O'Casey's *Silver Tassie* he had to take it off because his expenses were £1,700 a week.

.   .   .   .

"*Too True* failed, as they call it, in America also. That means that after twelve weeks' roaring business, the receipts dropped in the last week to $6,500. Well, if the vanguard of the drama cannot live on the drama when the plunder amounts to $6,500 a week, it must perish unless governments and municipalities come to the rescue with endowed theatres."

It is of interest to record that after the New York production Mr. Shaw had made a slight alteration in the play. He discovered that measles is not a microbe, and he thought of changing the nature of the disease from which the patient is suffering. Ernest Thesiger, who was playing the Monster, was so anxious to remain the "measles" that G. B. S. twisted the lines to suit the case. The Doctor explained:

"Patients insist on having microbes nowadays. If I told her there is no measles microbe she wouldn't believe me; and I should lose my patient. When there is no microbe I invent one."

Mr. Shaw wrote an article for the Malvern Festival Book, in which he made reference to the reception of the play by the American critics, who assumed that the "young gentleman-soldier-burglar-chaplain" was a mouth-piece of his own opinions, and informed their readers that he was finishing his life in a condition of disillusion and despair, having recanted all his professions, renounced all his convictions, abandoned all his hopes, and demolished all his Utopias.

"Many people are like that, both in America and here: if you hint that their country is not a paradise they call you a pessimist, though they never stop grumbling at the abominable way in which they are being treated by their own Governments. They also never tire of repeating that I point out evils without suggesting remedies, and am therefore not a practical man. Lest our English critics should start all that over again when they come down to Malvern—and many of them are quite capable of it—let me hasten to assure them that I have not recanted, renounced, abandoned nor demolished anything whatever, and that extremely practical and precise remedies, including a complete political reconstitution, a credible and scientific religion, and a satisfactory economic scheme, are discoverable by anyone under thirty (the older ones are past praying for) who will take the trouble to bring his or her education up to date by retiring into a House of Study and Contemplation and reading my works carefully through from beginning to end. I wrote them with a view to that; for though my trade is that of a playwright, my vocation is that of a prophet, with occasional lapses into what uncivil people call buffoonery. If my admirers dislike these lapses they should take care not to make me laugh, and to remember that there are others who think that I am endurable only when I indulge my unfortunate sense of humour.

"In Poland, where criticism seems better equipped culturally, the success of the play so terrified the authorities, that they sacked the censor who had, in deference to my reputation, passed the play without reading it. Do not, however, waste sympathy on this enlightened official: he was reinstated three days later, presumably to avert a pro-Shavian revolution; and the play was allowed to proceed subject to the excision of all the disparagements of war in the last act. I invite the attention of the League of Nations, and of all Pacifist leagues and conferences, to this gesture by the Polish Government, and the light it throws on the real views of Poland as to the moral respectability —not to say glory—of war. Not that I would suggest for a moment that those views are a jot different from the views of the other imperialist States; but none of them has been quite so candid about it as the Polish Government in this instance.

144

Design for the Lonely Wood, Act I,
in
" The Immortal Hour "

" The moral of my play, or rather the position illustrated by it, is simple enough. When wars were waged by professional armies, the reversal of morality which they involved was kept in a conscience-tight compartment: a civilian population might talk wickedly enough in its patriotic fervour; but it did not know what it was talking about: the actual slaughter and sack and rapine was only a story in the newspapers, not a real experience. But a war like that of 1914–1918, in which the whole male population of military age was forced to serve, hosts of women volunteered for work under fire, and the new feature of aerial bombardment brought the bloody part of the business crash into the civilians' bedrooms, was quite another matter. The shock to common morals was enormously greater and more general. So was the strain on the nerves. This time all the old romantic pretences of ' fearlessness' were dropped: nobody pretended to be immune either from acute funk under the barrage or from the wild reaction into security and hero-worship when at home on leave. When terror had gone to its limit, subse-quent indulgence for everything, from the pitch and toss of a night at *The Bing Boys* to the manslaughter of a correspondent, obeyed the law that action and reaction are equal. And so, for four years, it was taken as a matter of course that young people, when they were not under fire, must be allowed a good time.

" Now I do not at all object to young people having a good time. I think they should have a good time all the time, at peace as well as in war. I think that their having a good time is one of the tests of civilisation. But I very strenuously warn both young and old against the monstrous folly of supposing that a good time has any resemblance to those wartime reactions after paroxysms of horror and terror, when the most childish indulgence seemed heavenly and the most reckless excesses excusable on the plea of ' Let us eat and drink (especially drink); for to-morrow we die.' Our difficulty now is that what the bright young things after the war tried to do, and what their wretched survivors are still trying to do, is to get the reaction

145

without the terror, to go on eating cocaine and drinking cocktails as if they had only a few hours' expectation of life instead of forty years."

Somerset Maugham was at the first night of *Too True to be Good*, and somebody asked him the subject of his new play. He replied, " The same as Mr. Shaw's—this muddle of a post-war world." When it was produced at the Globe on November 1 *For Services Rendered* was found to be a relentless tragedy set in the household of a solicitor in a small town in Kent. Except perhaps in the portrait of the father, the note of irony—Mr. Maugham's accepted weapon—was missing. He presented a picture of the misery and frustration caused by the war—or rather the chaotic " peace " that the war years have left. The play is hard, bitter realism, and every one of the taut, chiselled lines in the dialogue left their mark and were part of the structure which reached its culmination in the terrible climax at the end.

Certain critics tempered their tributes to the dramatic power of the play by suggesting that the case had been overstated. It was a mistake, they said, to concentrate all that catastrophe in one quiet country household and to blame the war for everything that happened. There was a grain of truth in the criticisms, but no more. It is unnecessary to point out that drama is not life : it must simulate a framed picture of life, and Mr. Maugham, as a dramatic artist, claimed the artist's licence, and presented in the Ardsley household a microcosm of society as he sees it to-day.

It would be superfluous to say more about a play that is such recent history. The company was described by the author as the " most perfect cast " he had ever had in a play of his, and it would be invidious to mention individual performances when every part was so well played.

POSTSCRIPT

IF this book had been ready for publication in the autumn of 1932, at the end of the ten years' work in London, the final note would have been one of triumph. In October last it looked as if Barry Jackson would have three important productions running concurrently in London; that his faith in the real theatre had been vindicated. Instead, as this postscript goes to press, there is a prospect that he will cease temporarily from West-End management at the end of the run of the Somerset Maugham play, which was withdrawn from the Globe on December 17 and transferred to the Queen's with the same company a fortnight later, arrangements having been made for the production of *Evensong* to go to New York under the joint management of Arch Selwyn and Barry Jackson.

The fact that this postscript is necessary is further evidence of the hazards of the present-day theatre. Changes take place with dramatic suddenness, and it seems impossible to plan very far ahead. Since Barry Jackson brought *The Immortal Hour* to the Regent in 1922 he has produced over forty plays in London. A few of them were put on to meet the exigencies of the moment, but the majority of the productions demanded their place on the stage and cannot be overlooked when the history of the twentieth-century theatre is written.

It can be stated that only in one year during the whole of his career have Barry Jackson's collective theatrical ventures succeeded in yielding a profit, and then it was a comparatively small amount. His losses, on the other hand, have often been considerable. Those losses might have been much smaller if he had not felt himself irresistibly urged to foster such undertakings as the Birmingham Repertory Theatre and the Malvern Festival. It must be remembered that the Birmingham Theatre was built by him before the war and carefully planned to be selfsupporting. Economic conditions have, of course, undergone a radical change, and it is impossible to carry on the theatre satisfactorily without making a loss. The Malvern Festival, run as it is at present, is an idealistic venture which can never be made to pay its way.

We are concerned chiefly with London in this record, and of the productions included in the appendix only five have been financially successful: *The Farmer's Wife, Yellow Sands, The Apple Cart, The Barretts of Wimpole Street,* and *Evensong.* None of the others has shown a profit, and the majority have resulted in a loss.

It might be assumed that when there has been a pronounced success Barry Jackson has personally made a great deal of money. In view of the runs of *The Farmer's Wife, The Barretts of Wimpole Street,* and *The Apple Cart,* it would seem to be a fair deduction, and certainly the position at the end of any of the five successes would have been vastly different if he had been concerned with only one theatre. It must be remembered, however, that it is necessary to keep together a big organisation in order to prepare six plays annually for Malvern, send an expensive repertory to Canada, arrange for tours in England and run the Birmingham Repertory Theatre. The profitable plays have had to bear the heavy administrative expenses and the losses on the other aspects of Barry Jackson's work. It is doubtful whether any other theatrical organisation in this country maintains so many necessarily responsible employees on its permanent staff.

Barry Jackson has with some reluctance permitted the author to give these particulars, and then only to throw the limelight on theatrical conditions today. If he has any grievances they are emphatically not in any way tinged with selfpity, although he feels that the peculiar state of things at the present time is making the burden more than one man alone can justifiably bear. It cannot be too strongly insisted that his own case must not be confused with the singleaim project of running one WestEnd theatre.

He is as seriously concerned about the future as Mr. Shaw, who pointed out in the article quoted in the last chapter that *Too True to be Good* had to be withdrawn when it was taking £1,000 a week. It was not an unduly extravagant production, but to run it at that figure meant a weekly loss at the time the notice was given of two to three hundred pounds. He feels that there is something wrong when a play drawing that sum of money—which shows there were large numbers of people who wanted to see it—cannot be run on an economic basis.

The drama is a great and important art—perhaps the greatest, for it epitomises all the other arts. Yet it is handicapped all along the lines. Painting, sculpture, music, literature are in various ways subsidised by the Government, and instead of being helped, the theatre has to contribute to picture galleries and civil list pensions in the form of an entertainment tax. No exact figures are available, but, at a modest estimate, Barry Jackson has been responsible for the collection of £75,000 for the State. If (as he once said to Lady Snowden) he had put on rubbish he might have brought even more money into the National exchequer.

It is not the intention to finish this record with a plea for a National—or any other theatre. The facts stand. Barry Jackson's work is sufficiently well known; it has been accomplished in face of every sort of difficulty, and would have been still-born if he had not been a man of great wealth, great courage, and even greater energy. Running one or more West-End theatres is a long way from his ideal, which is a big self-supporting playhouse conducted on democratic lines at cheap prices with a permanent company and a catholic, constantly changing programme.

Whether it will ever be realised is another matter, but it is clear that managers, authors, actors, and theatre staffs must get together, face the existing problems, and adapt themselves to meet the changed conditions.

PROGRAMMES OF PLAYS

PRESENTED BY

BARRY JACKSON

THE IMMORTAL HOUR

BY RUTLAND BOUGHTON

Produced at the Regent Theatre on October 13, 1922

EOCHAIDH	W. JOHNSTONE-DOUGLAS
ETAIN	GWEN FFRANGCON-DAVIES
MIDIR	WILLIAM HESELTINE
DALUA	ARTHUR CRANMER
MANUS	HERBERT SIMMONDS
MAIVE	MARGARET CHATWIN
OLD BARD	HERBERT SIMMONDS
SPIRIT VOICE	DOROTHY D'ORSAY

PRODUCED BY
BARRY JACKSON

The costumes and scenery designed by PAUL SHELVING

THE CHRISTMAS PARTY

By Barry Jackson

Produced at the Regent Theatre on December 20, 1922

CHRISTOPHER	SIDNEY BROMLEY
EVANGELINE	KATHLEEN HEWITSON
NURSE	ALICE RENÉ
DUSTMAN	SCOTT SUNDERLAND
SANTA CLAUS	MARTIN SANDS
FINE LADY FROM BANBURY CROSS	MARGARET CHATWIN
BO PEEP	INA CARLETON
RED RIDING HOOD	DORIS DELORME
ANTHONY ROWLEY	IVOR BARNARD
CINDERELLA	MARJORIE BARTLETT
COLONEL MAC MASHIT	HEDLEY BRIGGS
THE LADY CLARA	CECILIA TWYFORD
GOLLYWOG	WILLIAM DEXTER
SAIRY JANE	CATHLEEN ORFORD
MR. NOAH	CHARLES STONE
MRS. NOAH	KATHLEEN BEER
NOAH'S LION	B. BRADLEY WILLIAMS
JACK-IN-THE-BOX	EDMUND HUMBERT
DICK WHITTINGTON	KENNETH SOLLY
HIS CAT	LEIGHTON LUCAS
ROBIN HOOD	CECIL PEARCE
MARY MARY	FAY YEATMAN

152

MISS MUFFET	DORIS PAGE
OLD KING COLE	CHARLES STONE
THE OLD WOMAN WHO LIVED IN A SHOE	ALICE RENÉ
THREE BLIND MICE ⎰	NANCY BYRNE
⎱	POPPY MISENER
. . . .	MARJORIE SHOOSMITH
CONJURER	JACK ROWLANDS
CLOWN	SCOTT SUNDERLAND
PANTALOON	IVOR BARNARD
HARLEQUIN	HEDLEY BRIGGS
COLUMBINE	CECILIA TWYFORD
FAIRY	JOAN PANTER

PRODUCER
H. K. AYLIFF

Costumes designed by GUY KORTRIGHT

THE IMMORTAL HOUR

By Rutland Boughton

Presented at the Regent Theatre on November 17, 1923

Eochaidh	W. JOHNSTONE-DOUGLAS
Etain	GWEN FFRANGCON-DAVIES
Midir	WILLIAM HESELTINE
Dalua	ARTHUR CRANMER
Manus	HERBERT SIMMONDS
Maive	DOROTHY D'ORSAY
Old Bard	HERBERT SIMMONDS
Spirit Voice	DOROTHY D'ORSAY

CONDUCTOR
APPLEBY MATTHEWS

PRODUCER
BARRY JACKSON

1st Revival

BETHLEHEM

BY RUTLAND BOUGHTON

Produced at the Regent Theatre on December 19, 1923

THE VIRGIN MARY	GWEN FFRANGCON-DAVIES
GABRIEL	COLIN ASHDOWN
JOSEPH	W. JOHNSTONE-DOUGLAS
THE THREE SHEPHERDS	HERBERT SIMMONDS
	KENNETH SOLLY
	EWART COOK
ANGELS	RUBY BOUGHTON
	MARJORIE BARTLETT
ZARATHUSTRA	ARTHUR CRANMER
NUBAR	TOM GOODEY
MERLIN	FREDERICK WOODHOUSE
WOMEN	MARGARET ARNOLD
	GRACE GEE
THE BELIEVER	NANCIE WILLIAMS
THE UNBELIEVER	HERBERT SIMMONDS
CALCHAS, THE HERALD	T. CREEGAN
HERODIAS	DOROTHY D'ORSAY
HEROD	FRANK TITTERTON

Production designed by BARRY JACKSON

THE IMMORTAL HOUR
By Rutland Boughton
Presented at the Regent Theatre on February 2, 1924

Eochaidh	W. JOHNSTONE-DOUGLAS
Etain	GWEN FFRANGCON-DAVIES
Midir	WILLIAM HESELTINE
Dalua	ARTHUR CRANMER
Manus	HERBERT SIMMONDS
Maive	DOROTHY D'ORSAY
Old Bard	HERBERT SIMMONDS
Spirit Voice	DOROTHY D'ORSAY

2nd Revival

156

BACK TO METHUSELAH

By Bernard Shaw

Produced at the Court Theatre on February 18, 1924

PART I

ADAM	COLIN KEITH-JOHNSTON
EVE	GWEN FFRANGCON-DAVIES
THE SERPENT	EDITH EVANS
CAIN	NIGEL CLARKE

PART II

FRANKLYN BARNABAS	WALLACE EVENNETT
CONRAD BARNABAS	FRANK MOORE
THE PARLOUR-MAID	CHRIS CASTOR
REV. WILLIAM HASLAM	CEDRIC HARDWICKE
SAVVY BARNABAS	EILEEN BELDON
JOYCE BURGE	MATTHEW BOULTON
LUBIN	CLIFFORD MARQUAND

PART III

BURGE-LUBIN	FRANK PETTINGELL
BARNABAS	FRANK MOORE
VOICE OF THE TELEPHONE OPERATOR	PHYLLIS SHAND
CONFUCIUS	PAUL SMYTHE
NEGRESS	EMMA WILLIAMS
THE ARCHBISHOP OF YORK	CEDRIC HARDWICKE
MRS. LUTESTRING	MARGARET CHATWIN

PART IV

THE ELDERLY GENTLEMAN	SCOTT SUNDERLAND
FUSIMA	MARGERY BRYCE
ZOZIM	RALPH RICHARDSON
ZOO	EILEEN BELDON

157

GENERAL AUFSTEIG (NAPOLEON)	.	.	MATTHEW BOULTON
THE ORACLE	.	.	. ESMÉ BERINGER
BADGER-BLUEBIN	.	.	. FRANK PETTINGELL
MRS. BADGER-BLUEBIN	.	.	. LUCIE EVELYN
MISS BADGER-BLUEBIN	.	.	PHYLLIS SHAND

PART V

STREPHON	.	.	GEORGE BLACKWOOD
CHLOE	.	.	. YVETTE PIENNE
HE-ANCIENT	.	.	CEDRIC HARDWICKE
ACIS	.	.	CECIL LANDEAU
SHE-ANCIENT	.	.	. EDITH EVANS
AMARYLLIS (THE NEWLY-BORN)	.	GWEN FFRANGCON-DAVIES
ECRASIA	.	.	. CHRIS CASTOR
ARJILLAX	.	.	STRINGER DAVIS
MARTELLUS	.	LAURENCE OLIVIER
PYGMALION	.	RALPH RICHARDSON
OZYMANDIAS	.	.	. NIGEL CLARKE
CLEOPATRA-SEMIRAMIS	.	AMY BRANDON-THOMAS
THE GHOST OF ADAM	.	COLIN KEITH-JOHNSTON
THE GHOST OF EVE	.	GWEN FFRANGCON-DAVIES
THE GHOST OF CAIN	.	.	. NIGEL CLARKE
THE GHOST OF THE SERPENT	.	.	. EDITH EVANS
LILITH	.	.	MARGARET CHATWIN

PRODUCER
H. K. AYLIFF

Scenery and costumes designed by PAUL SHELVING

THE FARMER'S WIFE

By Eden Phillpotts

Produced at the Court Theatre on March 11, 1924

CHURDLES ASH	CEDRIC HARDWICKE
ARAMINTA DENCH	EVELYN HOPE
THIRZA TAPPER	MAUD GILL
SAMUEL SWEETLAND	MELVILLE COOPER
SIBLEY SWEETLAND	PHYLLIS SHAND
GEORGE SMERDON	COLIN KEITH-JOHNSTON
PETRONELL SWEETLAND	EILEEN BELDON
RICHARD COAKER	SCOTT SUNDERLAND
LOUISA WINDEATT	MARGARET CHATWIN
SUSAN MAINE	IRIS KEMBER
SARAH SMERDON	AMY VENESS
SOPHIE SMERDON	BABY LOVE
TEDDY SMERDON	EVELYN TURNER
VALIANT DUNNYBRIG	PAUL SMYTHE
DR. RUNDLE	FRANK MOORE
MRS. RUNDLE	YVETTE PIENNE
HENRY COAKER	WALLACE EVENNETT
MARY HEARN	ISABEL THORNTON
THE REV. SEPTIMUS TUDOR	RAYMOND HUNTLEY
THE HON. MRS. TUDOR	FRANCES DOBLE

GLEE SINGERS
KENNETH SOLLY, LESLIE RODDA, BERTRAM D'ARCY, AND OSCAR
LANSBURY

PRODUCER
H. K. AYLIFF

Scenery and costumes designed by PAUL SHELVING

159

ROMEO AND JULIET
By William Shakespeare
Produced at the Regent Theatre on May 24, 1924

Escalus	GEORGE MANSHIP
Paris	REX O'MALLEY
Montague	GROSVENOR NORTH
Capulet	CHARLES VANE
An Old Man	PERCY ROBINSON
Romeo	JOHN GIELGUD
Mercutio	SCOTT SUNDERLAND
Benvolio	OSMUND WILLSON
Tybalt	ERIC LUGG
Friar Laurence	ERIC H. MESSITER
Friar John	WALTER SCHOFIELD
Balthasar	PERCY ROBINSON
Gregory	WALTER WALLIS
Peter	ERNEST G. COVE
Abraham	NOEL GOODWIN
An Apothecary	ERIC ALBURY
Chorus	GERALD JEROME
Page to Paris	GERALD ANDERSON
Another Page	HEDLEY BRIGGS
An Officer	ERIC SERLE
Lady Montague	CICELY OATES
Lady Capulet	MARIE HOUSLEY
Juliet	GWEN FFRANGCON-DAVIES
Nurse to Juliet	BARBARA GOTT

PRODUCER
H. K. AYLIFF

The costumes designed by PAUL SHELVING

160

CÆSAR AND CLEOPATRA

By Bernard Shaw

Produced at the Kingsway Theatre on April 21, 1925

THE GREAT GOD RA	LEWIN MANNERING
BELZANOR	REGINALD BESANT
A PERSIAN	ERIC MESSITER
A NUBIAN SENTINEL	J. A. BENTHAM
BEL AFFRIS	PHILIP DESBOROUGH
FTATATEETA	F. MARRIOTT WATSON
CLEOPATRA	GWEN FFRANGCON-DAVIES
CÆSAR	CEDRIC HARDWICKE
CENTURION	TERENCE O'BRIEN
POTHINUS	STANLEY LATHBURY
PTOLEMY	GERALD ANDERSON
THEODOTUS	ORLANDO BARNETT
ACHILLAS	PAUL SMYTHE
WOMAN OFFICIAL	AGNES IMLAY
RUFIO	FRANK MOORE
BRITANNUS	SCOTT SUNDERLAND
LUCIUS SEPTIMIUS	HOWIESON CULFF
WOUNDED ROMAN SOLDIER	HAROLD WRIGHT
ROMAN SENTINEL	DONALD FINLAY
APOLLODORUS	GEORGE HAYES
FIRST PORTER	J. E. MARTIN
BOATMAN	PAUL SMYTHE
CHARMIAN	HELEN SAINTSBURY
IRAS	MAY WARD
MUSICIAN	ERIC MESSITER
MAJOR DOMO	CHARLES LEIGHTON

PRODUCER
H. K. AYLIFF

Scenery, properties, and costumes designed by PAUL SHELVING

161

THE NEW MORALITY
By Harold Chapin

Produced at the Kingsway Theatre on June 29, 1925

BETTY JONES	GWEN FFRANGCON-DAVIES
LESCELINE	LOUISE DE LACY
ALICE MEYNE	FRANCES CLARE
COLONEL IVOR JONES	SCOTT SUNDERLAND
E. WALLACE WISTER	WALLACE EVENNETT
WOOTON	CEDRIC HARDWICKE
GEOFFREY BELASIS, K.C.	EDGAR NORFOLK

PRODUCER
H. K. AYLIFF

Scenery designed and executed in the Birmingham Repertory Theatre Workshops

HAMLET

By William Shakespeare

Produced at the Kingsway Theatre on August 15, 1925

CLAUDIUS	FRANK VOSPER
HAMLET	COLIN KEITH-JOHNSTON
POLONIUS	A. BROMLEY-DAVENPORT
HORATIO	ALAN HOWLAND
LAERTES	ROBERT HOLMES
VOLTIMAND	RUSSELL BARRY
ROSENCRANTZ	PATRICK WADDINGTON
OSRIC	GUY VIVIAN
GUILDENSTERN	WALTER HUDD
GHOST OF HAMLET'S FATHER	GROSVENOR NORTH
MARCELLUS	CYRIL VANE
BERNARDO	HAROLD W. WRIGHT
FIRST PLAYER	TERENCE O'BRIEN
SECOND PLAYER	NORMA VARDEN
FIRST GRAVEDIGGER	CEDRIC HARDWICKE
SECOND GRAVEDIGGER	H. M. BRADFORD
FORTINBRAS	DONALD FINLAY
GERTRUDE	DOROTHY MASSINGHAM
OPHELIA	MURIEL HEWITT

PRODUCER
H. K. AYLIFF

Scenery, costumes, properties designed by PAUL SHELVING

163

THE OLD ADAM

By Cicely Hamilton

Produced at the Kingsway Theatre on November 17, 1925

Mr. Shadlock	FEWLASS LLEWELLYN
Mr. Crawford	CLIFFORD MARQUAND
Mr. Barton-Phipps	CHARLES CARSON
General Cunliffe	SCOTT SUNDERLAND
Mr. Athelstane Lilley	GEORGE HOWE
Lieut. Robert Wilbraham	DOUGLAS HUTCHISON
Admiral Joe Bunting	ROY BYFORD
His Secretary	CARLETON HOBBS
The Bishop of Stephensbury	WILLIAM J. REA
The Siberian Ambassador	DRELINCOURT ODLUM
A Clerk at the War Office	GEOFFREY WILKINSON
A Messenger at the War Office	HEDLEY BRIGGS
Rawlinson	CHARLES LEIGHTON
Betty Cunliffe	FRANCES CLARE
Miss Hildegarde Jones, M.D., M.R.C.S.	OLGA SLADE

PRODUCER
H. K. AYLIFF

Scenery designed by PAUL SHELVING

164

THE IMMORTAL HOUR
By Rutland Boughton

Presented at the Kingsway Theatre on January 30, 1926

EOCHAIDH	W. JOHNSTONE-DOUGLAS
ETAIN	GWEN FFRANGCON-DAVIES
MIDIR	WILLIAM HESELTINE
DALUA	ARTHUR CRANMER
MANUS	HERBERT SIMMONDS
MAIVE	DOROTHY D'ORSAY
OLD BARD	HERBERT SIMMONDS
SPIRIT VOICE	DOROTHY D'ORSAY

3rd Revival

THE MARVELLOUS HISTORY OF ST. BERNARD

By Henri Ghéon

Produced at the Kingsway Theatre on April 7, 1926

FOOL	. DENNIS BARRY
BERNARD	. ROBERT HARRIS
RICHARD OF MENTHON	SCOTT SUNDERLAND
DAME BERNOLINE	. MARGARET CHATWIN
SEIGNEUR DE DUYNGT	. ERNEST HAINES
SEIGNEUR DE BIAUFORT	. PETER CRESWELL
MASTER GERMAIN	. ANDREW CHURCHMAN
MENTHON (THE HERALD)	. JAMES DALE
MINSTREL	. LAURENCE OLIVIER
JOSEPHINE	DAISY ENGLAND
MARGUERITE	GWEN FFRANGCON-DAVIES
SEIGNEUR DE MIOLANS	. CHARLES MAUNSELL
THE LADY DE MIOLANS	. ESME HUBBARD
MIOLANS (THE HERALD)	. GEORGE HOWE
CASTOR	. LESLIE PAINE
PRIOR OF AOSTA	. H. O. NICHOLSON
PORTER OF THE MONASTERY	. ALAN EDMISTON
BONAVENTURE (THE 10TH PILGRIM)	. OSMUND WILLSON
OUR LADY	. VALERIE TAYLOR
ST. GABRIEL	. DENYS BLAKELOCK
ST. NICHOLAS	GROSVENOR NORTH
SATAN	. CHARLES MAUNSELL
MURDER	. NOEL GOODWIN
PRIDE	. M. S. MOTTRAM
ENVY	. HEDLEY BRIGGS
GLUTTONY	. ALAN EDMISTON

PRODUCER
A. E. FILMER

Costumes and scenery designed by PAUL SHELVING

166

ROSMERSHOLM

BY HENRIK IBSEN

ENGLISH VERSION BY R. FARQUHARSON SHARP

Produced at the Kingsway Theatre on September 30, 1926

JOHN ROSMER	CHARLES CARSON
REBECCA WEST	EDITH EVANS
JAMES CROWLEY	RUPERT HARVEY
ERIC BRENDON	ROBERT FARQUHARSON
ALFRED ROBINSON	GEORGE HOWE
MARTHA	MURIEL AKED

PRODUCER
H. K. AYLIFF

Scenery designed by PAUL SHELVING

YELLOW SANDS

By Eden and Adelaide Phillpotts

Produced at the Haymarket Theatre on November 3, 1926

RICHARD VARWELL	CEDRIC HARDWICKE
EMMA MAJOR	VIOLA LYEL
ARTHUR VARWELL	RALPH RICHARDSON
JOE VARWELL	FRANK VOSPER
MR. BASLOW	H. O. NICHOLSON
THOMAS MAJOR	EDWARD PETLEY
LYDIA BLAKE	MURIEL HEWITT
MARY VARWELL	AMY VENESS
JENIFER VARWELL	SUSAN RICHMOND
MINNIE MASTERS	ALICE WILLS
NELLY MASTERS	DRUSILLA WILLS

PRODUCER
H. K. AYLIFF

The scenery designed by PAUL SHELVING

THE DESPERATE LOVERS
By Alfred Sutro

Produced at the Comedy Theatre on January 28, 1927

Miss Enticknap	. . . . GWYNEDD VERNON
Mrs. Bailey-Parker	. . . . HELEN HAYE
The Baroness della Rocca	. . . . . . IRENE VANBRUGH
Mellish	. . . . FRANK LACY
Alexander Duminy	. . . . ALLAN AYNESWORTH
Mr. Seed	. . . . FEWLASS LLEWELLYN
Enid Bassopp	. . . . EILEEN BELDON
Marshall	. . . . A. W. BEALE
Everard Bassopp	. . . . SCOTT SUNDERLAND
Lady Eulalie Havers	. . . . MARDA VANNE
Mr. Bulger	. . . . AUBREY MALLALIEU

PRODUCER
H. K. AYLIFF

Scenery designed by PAUL SHELVING

THE BLUE COMET

By Eden Phillpotts

Produced at the Court Theatre on February 23, 1927

MARY PARSONS	MINNIE RAYNER
JAMES PARSONS	ELIOT MAKEHAM
NICHOLAS BEDALE	GEORGE ELTON
MILLICENT BEDALE	CECILY BYRNE
JANE BEDALE	DOROTHY HALL
ELIZABETH BEDALE	DOROTHY BLACK
COLONEL LUCAS BEDALE, V.C., C.B.	CLARENCE BLAKISTON
MORRIS BEDALE	EDWARD CHAPMAN
CHRISTOPHER BEDALE	PAUL CAVANAGH

PRODUCER
H. K. AYLIFF

Scenery designed by PAUL SHELVING

BERT'S GIRL

By Elizabeth Baker

Produced at the Court Theatre on March 30, 1927

MRS. WALTERS	MINNIE RAYNER
BERT	HENRY CAINE
BASIL	A. J. DENTON
IRIS	NADINE MARCH
EVELYN	PHYLLIS PERCY
STELLA MARSH	DOROTHY BLACK
DAISY	MARJORIE LARCOMBE
MRS. TATT	MADGE TRENCHARD
EDGAR TATT	EDWARD CHAPMAN
MARTIN TRENT	JULIAN D'ALBIE
JOHN PUTTOCK	WILSON COLEMAN
STEPHEN QUINTON	GEORGE BLACKWOOD

PRODUCER

H. K. AYLIFF

Scenery designed and painted by PAUL SHELVING

THE ADDING MACHINE
By Elmer Rice

Produced at the Court Theatre on January 9, 1928

Mr. Zero	FRANK RANDELL
Mrs. Zero	CARRIE BAILLIE
Daisy Diana Dorothea Devore	DOROTHY TURNER
The Boss	PHILIP HEWLAND
Mr. One	PHILIP HEWLAND
Mrs. One	MARGARET CHATWIN
Mr. Two	LEONARD CALVERT
Mrs. Two	ELEANOR GARLAND
Mr. Three	ROBERT LANG
Mrs. Three	DOROTHY PAGET
Mr. Four	PERCY RHODES
Mrs. Four	JEAN STURROCK
Mr. Five	HOWELL DAVIES
Mrs. Five	CHRISTINE MORGAN
Mr. Six	BASIL DYNE
Mrs. Six	STELLA CAMBERIAN
Policeman	ALFRED W. BEALE
Judy O'Grady	BEATRIX LEHMANN
Young Man	LAURENCE OLIVIER
Shrdlu	CHARLES MAUNSELL
A Head	HOWELL DAVIES
Lieutenant Charles	PERCY RHODES
Joe	ROBERT LANG

PRODUCER
W. G. FAY

Scenery and costumes designed by HUGH OWEN

172

MACBETH

By William Shakespeare

Produced at the Court Theatre on February 6, 1928

Duncan	CYRIL JERVIS-WALTER
Malcolm	LAURENCE OLIVIER
Donaldbain	IVAN BRANDT
Macbeth	ERIC MATURIN
Banquo	MARSHALL SHEPPARD
Macduff	SCOTT SUNDERLAND
Lennox	HOWARD COCHRAN
Ross	NIGEL CLARKE
Menteith	GEORGE BLACKWOOD
Angus	MARTYN ROLAND
Caithness	WALLACE EVENNETT
Fleance	W. E. C. JENKINS
Siward	JAMES CARRALL
Young Siward, his Son	ANTONY EUSTREL
Seyton	FRANK MOORE
Boy, Son to Macduff	COLIN CARDEW
A Doctor	PAUL SMYTHE
A Sergeant	A. GILLETTE
Porter	FRANK PETTINGELL
An Old Man	FRANK MACRAE
First Murderer	DOUGLAS PAYNE
Second Murderer	ERNEST STIDWELL

SERVANTS, ATTENDING ON MACBETH $\left\{\begin{array}{l} . \quad . \quad . \quad . \quad . \quad . \quad \text{FRANCIS DRAKE} \\ . \quad . \quad . \quad \text{ALEXANDER CUNNINGHAM} \\ . \quad . \quad . \quad . \quad . \quad . \quad \text{CYRIL FAIRLIE} \end{array}\right.$

LADY MACBETH . . . . MARY MERRALL

LADY MACDUFF . . . . CHRIS CASTOR

GENTLEWOMAN, ATTENDING ON LADY MACBETH . . . . . EILEEN BELDON

FIRST WITCH . . . . MURIEL AKED

SECOND WITCH . . . . JOAN PEREIRA

THIRD WITCH . . . . UNA O'CONNOR

APPARITIONS $\left\{\begin{array}{l} . \quad . \quad . \quad . \quad . \quad . \quad \text{ALEXANDER CUNNINGHAM} \\ . \quad . \quad . \quad . \quad . \quad . \quad . \quad \text{ELSIE CLARK} \\ . \quad . \quad . \quad . \quad . \quad . \quad . \quad \text{LESLIE PAIN} \end{array}\right.$

PRODUCER
H. K. AYLIFF

Scenery designed by PAUL SHELVING

THE THIRD FINGER

By R. R. Whittaker

Produced at the Everyman Theatre on February 6, 1928

Angelica Stannard	ISABEL THORNTON
Clarissa Stannard	MAUD GILL
Fanny Marshall	FREDA CLARK
Phil Hardcastle	ROLAND CULVER
Susan Whorlow	OLGA MURGATROYD
Tom Hardcastle	CECIL LANDEAU
Marion Stannard	LILA MARAVAN
Charles S. Smith-Weston	MELVILLE COOPER
The Rev. Francis Gresham	ERIC MESSITER
Maid at the Vicarage	HYLDA MILES
The Misses Stannard's Maid	JOSETTE MacSHERRY

PRODUCER
W. G. FAY

BACK TO METHUSELAH

By Bernard Shaw

Presented at the Court Theatre on March 5, 1928

PART I

ADAM	COLIN KEITH-JOHNSTON
EVE	GWEN FFRANGCON-DAVIES
THE SERPENT	EDITH EVANS
CAIN	NIGEL CLARKE

PART II

FRANKLYN BARNABAS	WALLACE EVENNETT
CONRAD BARNABAS	FRANK MOORE
THE PARLOUR-MAID	CHRIS CASTOR
REV. WILLIAM HASLAM	CEDRIC HARDWICKE
SAVVY BARNABAS	EILEEN BELDON
JOYCE BURGE	MATTHEW BOULTON
LUBIN	CLIFFORD MARQUAND

PART III

BURGE-LUBIN	FRANK PETTINGELL
BARNABAS	FRANK MOORE
VOICE OF THE TELEPHONE OPERATOR	PHYLLIS SHAND
CONFUCIUS	PAUL SMYTHE
NEGRESS	EMMA WILLIAMS
THE ARCHBISHOP OF YORK	CEDRIC HARDWICKE
MRS. LUTESTRING	MARGARET CHATWIN

176

PART IV

THE ELDERLY GENTLEMAN	SCOTT SUNDERLAND
FUSIMA	MARGERY BRYCE
ZOZIM	RALPH RICHARDSON
ZOO	EILEEN BELDON
GENERAL AUFSTEIG (NAPOLEON)	MATTHEW BOULTON
THE ORACLE	ESMÉ BERINGER
BADGER-BLUEBIN	FRANK PETTINGELL
MRS. BADGER-BLUEBIN	LUCIE EVELYN
MISS BADGER-BLUEBIN	PHYLLIS SHAND

PART V

STREPHON	GEORGE BLACKWOOD
CHLOE	YVETTE PIENNE
HE-ANCIENT	CEDRIC HARDWICKE
ACIS	CECIL LANDEAU
SHE-ANCIENT	EDITH EVANS
AMARYLLIS (THE NEWLY-BORN)	GWEN FFRANGCON-DAVIES
ECRASIA	CHRIS CASTOR
ARJILLAX	STRINGER DAVIS
MARTELLUS	LAURENCE OLIVIER
PYGMALION	RALPH RICHARDSON
OZYMANDIAS	NIGEL CLARKE
CLEOPATRA-SEMIRAMIS	AMY BRANDON-THOMAS
THE GHOST OF ADAM	COLIN KEITH-JOHNSTON
THE GHOST OF EVE	GWEN FFRANGCON-DAVIES
THE GHOST OF CAIN	NIGEL CLARKE
THE GHOST OF THE SERPENT	EDITH EVANS
LILITH	MARGARET CHATWIN

PRODUCER
H. K. AYLIFF

Scenery and costumes designed by PAUL SHELVING

177

HAROLD

By Alfred, Lord Tennyson

Produced at the Court Theatre on April 2, 1928

PROLOGUE
GWEN FFRANGCON-DAVIES

King Edward the Confessor	GEORGE HOWE
Stigand	CLIFFORD MARQUAND
Alfred	WALLACE EVENNETT
Bishop of London	FRANCIS DRAKE
Harold	LAURENCE OLIVIER
Tostig	ROBERT SPEAIGHT
Gurth	RALPH RICHARDSON
Leofwin	STRINGER DAVIS
Wulfnoth	W. E. C. JENKINS
Morcar	FRANK MOORE
Edwin	IVAN BRANDT
Gamel	FRANK PETTINGELL
Court Ladies {	CHRIS CASTOR
	LUCIE EVELYN
	PHYLLIS SHAND
Attendant on Harold	CECIL LANDEAU
An Old Thane	ERNEST STIDWELL
First Thane	PAUL SMYTHE
Thane from Pevensey	FRANCIS DRAKE
Osgod	CECIL LANDEAU

178

ATHELRIC	FRANK MACRAE
COUNT WILLIAM OF NORMANDY	SCOTT SUNDERLAND
WILLIAM MALET	NIGEL CLARKE
GUY, COUNT OF PONTHIEU	ANTONY EUSTREL
HUGH MARGOT	ERNEST STIDWELL
A NORMAN OFFICER	PAUL SMYTHE
	FRANK BURDEN
MEN-AT-ARMS	HUGH BARNES
	ALEXANDER CUNNINGHAM
ROLF	NORMAN CLARIDGE
A FISHERMAN	FRANK MACRAE
A NORMAN SAINT	BETTY WILLIAMSON
THE QUEEN	MARGARET CHATWIN
ALDWYTH	EILEEN BELDON
EDITH	GWEN FFRANGCON-DAVIES

PRODUCER
H. K. AYLIFF

Scenery and costumes designed by PAUL SHELVING

BIRD IN HAND

By John Drinkwater

Produced at the Royalty Theatre on April 18, 1928

Joan Greenleaf	JILL ESMOND MOORE
Alice Greenleaf	AMY VENESS
Thomas Greenleaf	HERBERT LOMAS
Gerald Arnwood	PATRICK SUSANDS
Mr. Blanquet	IVOR BARNARD
Cyril Beverley	CHARLES MAUNSELL
Ambrose Godolphin, K.C.	FELIX AYLMER
Sir Robert Arnwood	FRANK ALLENBY

PRODUCER
JOHN DRINKWATER

Scenery designed by HUGH OWEN

THE TAMING OF THE SHREW

By William Shakespeare

Produced at the Court Theatre on April 30, 1928

PERSONS IN THE INDUCTION

CHRISTOPHER SLY	FRANK PETTINGELL
HOSTESS	LUCIE EVELYN
A LORD	LAURENCE OLIVIER
GUESTS	MARGERY BRYCE
	BETTY WILLIAMSON
	FRANK BURDEN
SERVANTS	PAUL SMYTHE
	FRANCIS DRAKE
	NORMAN CLARIDGE
PAGE	CHARLES LAMB
HUNT SERVANTS	ERNEST STIDWELL
	FRANK MACRAE

PERSONS IN THE PLAY

BAPTISTA	CLIFFORD MARQUAND
VINCENTIO	FRANK MOORE
LUCENTIO	NIGEL CLARKE
PETRUCHIO	SCOTT SUNDERLAND
A PEDANT	ERNEST STIDWELL
A TAILOR	ANTONY EUSTREL
GREMIO	WALLACE EVENNETT
HORTENSIO	RONALD SIMPSON
TRANIO	RALPH RICHARDSON
BIONDELLO	WILYM JENKINS
GRUMIO	EDWARD CHAPMAN
CURTIS	DRUSILLA WILLS
KATHARINA	EILEEN BELDON
BIANCA	MURIEL HEWITT
WIDOW	CHRIS CASTOR

PRODUCER

H. K. AYLIFF

Scenery designed by PAUL SHELVING

181

SIX CHARACTERS IN SEARCH OF AN AUTHOR

FROM THE ITALIAN OF LUIGI PIRANDELLO

English version by H. K. AYLIFF

Produced at the Arts Theatre Club on May 20, 1928

THE CHARACTERS

THE FATHER	WALTER PEARCE
THE MOTHER	MARGARET CHATWIN
THE STEPDAUGHTER	DOROTHY BLACK
THE SON	COLIN KEITH-JOHNSTON
THE LITTLE BOY	JOHN DENIS
THE LITTLE GIRL	BETTY RAYMOND
MME PEACE	ISABEL THORNTON

THE COMPANY

THE MANAGER AND PRODUCER	FEWLASS LLEWELLYN
THE LEADING LADY	DOROTHY HOLMES-GORE
THE LEADING MAN	D. A. CLARKE-SMITH
THE CHARACTER LADY	MADGE BURBAGE
THE INGÉNUE	DOROTHY REVELLY
THE LIGHT COMEDY LADY	ETHEL O'SHEA
THE JUVENILE MAN	PHILIP EASTON
THE CHARACTER MAN	VICTOR LUSK
THE STAGE-MANAGER	MATTHEW FORSYTH
THE ASSISTANT STAGE-MANAGER	FRANK IRISH, JUN.
THE MASTER CARPENTER	CHARLES LEIGHTON
THE PROPERTY MASTER	KINGSTONE TROLLOPE
THE STAGE DOOR-KEEPER	JULIAN D'ALBIE

PRODUCER
H. K. AYLIFF

182

SIX CHARACTERS IN SEARCH OF AN AUTHOR

FROM THE ITALIAN OF LUIGI PIRANDELLO

English version by H. K. AYLIFF

Produced at the Globe Theatre on May 28, 1928

THE COMPANY

THE MANAGER AND PRODUCER	FEWLASS LLEWELLYN
THE LEADING LADY	DOROTHY HOLMES-GORE
THE HEAVY LADY	IVY DES VOEUX
THE CHARACTER LADY	MADGE BURBAGE
THE GRANDE DAME	WINNIE TEMPEST
THE INGÉNUE	DOROTHY REAVELEY
THE LIGHT COMEDY LADY	ETHEL O'SHEA
THE SOUBRETTE	BETTY WILLIAMSON
THE LEADING MAN	D. A. CLARKE-SMITH
THE JUVENILE MAN	PHILIP EASTON
THE CHARACTER MAN	ERNEST HAINES
THE SECOND JUVENILE MAN	NORMAN CLARIDGE
THE STAGE-MANAGER	JULIAN D'ALBIE
THE ASSISTANT STAGE-MANAGER	FRANK IRISH, JUN.
THE MASTER CARPENTER	CHARLES LEIGHTON
THE PROPERTY MASTER	KINGSTONE TROLLOPE
THE STAGE DOOR-KEEPER	A. CATON-WOODVILLE

THE CHARACTERS

THE FATHER	WALTER PEARCE
THE MOTHER	MARGARET CHATWIN
THE STEPDAUGHTER	DOROTHY BLACK
THE SON	COLIN KEITH-JOHNSTON
THE BOY	JOHN DENIS
THE LITTLE GIRL	BETTY RAYMOND
MADAME PEACE	ISABEL THORNTON

PRODUCER
H. K. AYLIFF

THE FARMER'S WIFE

By Eden Phillpotts

Presented at the Court Theatre on July 17, 1928

Churdles Ash	ERNEST STIDWELL
Araminta Dench	DOROTHY DARKE
Thirza Tapper	CICELY OATES
Samuel Sweetland	FREDERICK VICTOR
Sibley Sweetland	KIRSTY MACKINTOSH
George Smerdon	CYRIL RENISON
Petronell Sweetland	MARGARET GRIMSDALE
Richard Coaker	EDMUND TOTTENHAM
Louisa Windeatt	JANET HODSON
Valiant Dunnybrig	FRANK LACY
Henry Coaker	VICTOR LUSK
Mary Hearn	FRANCES DAVIE

(Visit of touring company)

AREN'T WOMEN WONDERFUL!

By Harris Deans

Produced at the Court Theatre on August 14, 1928

Con Hawley	DOROTHY TURNER
Ben Hawley	RALPH RICHARDSON
Florrie	KATHLEEN HARRISON
Forbes Johnstone	GEORGE BARRETT
Mr. Jackman	EDWARD CHAPMAN
Rhoda Johnstone	ISABEL THORNTON
Henry Satterwaite	CLIFFORD MARQUAND
Irene Satterwaite	DOROTHY HOLMES-GORE
Mr. Curtis	HORACE HUNTER
"Felix" Strelitzki	ANTONY EUSTREL

PRODUCER
H. K. AYLIFF

Scenery designed by PAUL SHELVING

THE RUNAWAYS

By Eden Phillpotts

Produced at the Garrick Theatre on November 14, 1928

Benjamin Borlase	H. O. NICHOLSON
Matthew Borlase	SAM LIVESEY
Albert Borlase	COLIN KEITH-JOHNSTON
Jessie Borlase	EILEEN BELDON
Keturah Borlase	ISABEL THORNTON
Gladys Wonnacott	MURIEL HEWITT
James Jago	RALPH RICHARDSON
Harold Widger	BEN FIELD
Eliza Widger	DOROTHY HALL

PRODUCER
H. K. AYLIFF

Scenery designed by PAUL SHELVING

THE MAYOR

By Adelaide Phillpotts

Produced at the Royalty Theatre on March 11, 1929

Miss Virginia Whitehead	CICELY OATES
Ivy	BEE ARCHDALE
Mr. Paul Graham	NORMAN CLARIDGE
Mrs. Twigg	DOROTHY HALL
Mr. Hopkins	WILFRED E. BRANDON
Mrs. Carpenter	MARGARET CHATWIN
Dr. Carpenter	FRED RIVENHALL
Miss Bertha Beck, O.B.E.	EILEEN BELDON
Mrs. Barton-Abbott	ISABEL THORNTON
Miss Vera Barton-Abbott	PAULA SABINA
Mr. Theodore Bartlett	PHILIP EASTON
Admiral Sir James Copley-Trenchard	JULIAN D'ALBIE
Lady Henrietta Copley-Trenchard	MARGERY BRYCE
Miss Jane Cooper	ANN BROWN
Colonel Arthur Maddison	CLIFFORD MARQUAND
Mr. William Bowden	WILLIAM HEILBRONN
Mrs. Bowden	LUCIE EVELYN
Miss Patricia Bowden	EILEEN SHAND

PRODUCER
H. K AYLIFF

Scenery designed by PAUL SHELVING

187

THE APPLE CART

By Bernard Shaw

Produced at the Queen's Theatre on September 17, 1929

PAMPHILIUS	WALLACE EVENNETT
SEMPRONIUS	SCOTT SUNDERLAND
BOANERGES	MATTHEW BOULTON
MAGNUS	CEDRIC HARDWICKE
PROTEUS	CHARLES CARSON
NICOBAR	CLIFFORD MARQUAND
CRASSUS	JULIAN D'ALBIE
PLINY	AUBREY MALLALIEU
BALBUS	FRANK MOORE
AMANDA	DOROTHY HOLMES-GORE
LYSISTRATA	EILEEN BELDON
ORINTHIA	EDITH EVANS
QUEEN JEMIMA	BARBARA EVEREST
THE PRINCESS ROYAL	EVE TURNER
MR. VANHATTAN	JAMES CAREW

PRODUCER

H. K. AYLIFF

Scenery and costumes designed by PAUL SHELVING

THE SHADOWS OF STRIFE
BY JOHN DAVISON

Produced at the Arts Theatre Club on December 8, 1929

MRS. BREWSTER	CICELY OATES
LUKE BREWSTER	KENNETH FRAZER
MATTHEW MERRIDEW	CEDRIC HARDWICKE
GEORGE BREWSTER	WILLIAM HEILBRONN
JOHN BREWSTER	NORMAN CLARIDGE
MARY BREWSTER	DAPHNE HEARD
MRS. FLOWITT	ISABEL THORNTON
A CHILD	PHYLLIS SHAND
MR. DONALDSON	PAUL SMYTHE
INSPECTOR BROADHEAD	HOWELL DAVIES
SNOWBALL BATES	HARRY WILCOXON
A MAN	HUGH MOXEY

PRODUCER
H. K. AYLIFF

Scenery designed by PAUL SHELVING

189

THE WHITE ASSEGAI

By Allan King

Produced at the Playhouse on January 21, 1930

M'Buru	RONALD BUCHANAN
Inyoga	WILFRED E. BRANDON
Jenny Nichol	DAPHNE HEARD
Helen Mackenzie	MINNIE BLAGDEN
Hardress Mackenzie	GODFREY TEARLE
Nicholas Mackenzie	HARRY WILCOXON
Doctor MacAndrew	ERNEST THESIGER
Machado	WILLIAM HEILBRONN
M'Sanga	HOWELL DAVIES
Giles	NORMAN CLARIDGE
Susie	PHYLLIS SHAND
Charlie	BARRY K. BARNES
Johannes van den Bergh	ARTHUR CHISHOLM
Mrs. van den Bergh (Tante Anna)	MARIANNE CALDWELL

PRODUCER
H. K. AYLIFF

Scenery designed by PAUL SHELVING

190

DEVONSHIRE CREAM

BY EDEN PHILLPOTTS

Produced at the Playhouse on February 13, 1930

ELIAS WIDECOMBE	SAM LIVESEY
AMY WIDECOMBE	MARY JERROLD
BETH WIDECOMBE	PHYLLIS SHAND
WILLIAM BLEE	HORACE HODGES
GREGORY SWEET	NORMAN CLARIDGE
JENNY SWEET	DAPHNE HEARD
JOSEPH MUNDAY	H. O. NICHOLSON
ROBERT BLANCHARD	HARRY WILCOXON

PRODUCER
H. K. AYLIFF

Scenery designed by PAUL SHELVING

THE BARRETTS OF WIMPOLE STREET
BY RUDOLF BESIER

Produced at the Queen's Theatre on September 23, 1930

DOCTOR CHAMBERS	AUBREY MALLALIEU
ELIZABETH BARRETT MOULTON-BARRETT	GWEN FFRANGCON-DAVIES
WILSON	EILEEN BELDON
HENRIETTA MOULTON-BARRETT	MARJORIE MARS
ARABEL MOULTON-BARRETT	SUSAN RICHMOND
OCTAVIUS MOULTON-BARRETT	BARRY K. BARNES
SEPTIMUS MOULTON-BARRETT	BRYAN COLEMAN
ALFRED MOULTON-BARRETT	HUGH MOXEY
CHARLES MOULTON-BARRETT	LEONARD BENNETT
HENRY MOULTON-BARRETT	DOUGLAS QUAYLE
GEORGE MOULTON-BARRETT	ANTHONY MARSHALL
EDWARD MOULTON-BARRETT	CEDRIC HARDWICKE
BELLA HEDLEY	JOAN BARRY
HENRY BEVAN	OLIVER JOHNSTON
ROBERT BROWNING	SCOTT SUNDERLAND
DOCTOR FORD-WATERLOW	WILFRED CAITHNESS
CAPTAIN SURTEES COOK	HARRY WILCOXON
FLUSH	TUPPENNY OF WARE

PRODUCER
H. K. AYLIFF

Costumes and scenery designed by PAUL SHELVING

192

JANE'S LEGACY

BY EDEN PHILLPOTTS

Produced at the Duchess Theatre, December 16, 1930

IVY MORTIMORE	VIOLA LYEL
JACK MORTIMORE	FRANK MOORE
SERGEANT MERRYWEATHER CHUGG	FRANK PETTINGELL
JOHN FORD	COLIN KEITH-JOHNSTON
NED THORN	PAUL KELSTON
MRS. SUSAN THORN	BARBARA GOTT
EMMELINE COODE	LESLEY COX
JANE MORTIMORE	LOUISE HAMPTON
TOM SPARROW	HENRY CAINE
SAMUEL	HERBERT LUGG
DAISY FORD	KATHLEEN HARRISON
RUPERT SPARROW	NORMAN CLARIDGE
THE REV. PHILIP RYLE	STANLEY NEWMAN
THE 'AND OF PROVIDENCE	DOROTHY HALL

PRODUCER
H. K. AYLIFF

Scenery and ladies' costumes designed by PAUL SHELVING

193

DEMOS, KING AND SLAVE

By Henri Ghéon

Adapted into English by Barry Jackson
Verses translated by John Drinkwater

Produced at the Arts Theatre Club on July 1, 1931

PROLOGUE

Chorus of Old Men	PASCOE THORNTON
	CLEMENT HAMELIN
	A. CATON-WOODVILLE
	A. CORNEY GRAIN
	DOUGLAS PHAIR
	FRANCIS HOPE
Poet	WALTER HUDD

PLAY

Demos	ANDREW LEIGH
His Wife	AMY VENESS
Cousin Bung	DEREK COTTER
Cleon	JULIAN D'ALBIE
Plautus	JOHN H. MOORE
Nicias	WILLIAM FAZAN
The Political Muse	AGNES LAUCHLAN
Postman	KINGSTONE TROLLOPE
A Grocer	PASCOE THORNTON
A Restaurant Keeper	A. CATON-WOODVILLE

194

A Bootblack	REGINALD BROOKE
A Young Red Cousin	RICHARD SEATON
Another Red Cousin	F. THORNTON-BASSETT
A Stranger	CLEMENT HAMELIN
The Goddess of War	JEANNE GARMAN
A Young Man	WALTER HUDD
Themistocles	A. CORNEY GRAIN
Watchman	FRANCIS HOPE

PRODUCER
MATTHEW FORSYTH

Setting designed by H. BLACKMAR DASH

A TRIP TO SCARBOROUGH

By Sir John Vanbrugh and Richard Brinsley Sheridan

Produced at St. James's Theatre on September 14, 1931

PROLOGUE SPOKEN BY GROSVENOR NORTH

Lord Foppington	ERNEST THESIGER
Young Fashion	HARRY WILCOXON
Loveless	ROBERT DONAT
Colonel Townly	EDGAR NORFOLK
Sir Tunbelly Clumsy	ERIC STANLEY
Probe	FRANK MOORE
Lory	LESLIE HOLLAND
La Varole	SIDNEY RENNEF
Postilion	NORMAN WELCH
Shoemaker	CHARLES LEIGHTON
Tailor	HOWELL DAVIES
Hosier	CHARLES CHILDERSTONE
Jeweller	JACK CARLTON
Lord Foppington's Footmen {	TONY BRUCE
	DONALD ECCLES
Sir Tunbelly's Servants {	CHARLES LEIGHTON
	SIDNEY RENNEF
Constable	HOWELL DAVIES
Berinthia	FRANCES CARSON
Amanda	GILLIAN LIND
Mrs. Coupler	MARGARET CHATWIN

NURSE . . . . ISABEL THORNTON

SEMPSTRESS . . . . LUCIE EVELYN

AMANDA'S MAID . . . . ANNE KASMIR

BERINTHIA'S MAID . . . . PEGGY MORTON

MISS HOYDEN . . . . MIRIAM ADAMS

EPILOGUE SPOKEN BY "LORD FOPPINGTON"

PRODUCER
H. K. AYLIFF

The scenery, costumes and properties designed by PAUL SHELVING

THE FARMER'S WIFE
BY EDEN PHILLPOTTS

Presented at the Queen's Theatre on January 5, 1932

CHURDLES ASH	CEDRIC HARDWICKE
ARAMINTA DENCH	EVELYN HOPE
THIRZA TAPPER	MAUD GILL
SAMUEL SWEETLAND	MELVILLE COOPER
SIBLEY SWEETLAND	PHYLLIS SHAND
GEORGE SMERDON	NORMAN CLARIDGE
PETRONELL SWEETLAND	EILEEN BELDON
RICHARD COAKER	ROGER LIVESEY
LOUISA WINDEATT	MARGARET CHATWIN
SUSAN MAINE	MARGARET LARCOMBE
SARAH SMERDON	AMY VENESS
SOPHIE SMERDON	PAT LEVEAUX
TEDDY SMERDON	GLADYS GILBERT
VALIANT DUNNYBRIG	DOUGLAS PAYNE
MRS. RUNDLE	FLORENCE LECLERCQ
DR. RUNDLE	FRANK MOORE
HENRY COAKER	FRED PERMAIN
MARY HEARN	ISABEL THORNTON
THE REV. SEPTIMUS TUDOR	RAYMOND HUNTLEY
THE HON. MRS. TUDOR	ANNE WILSON

GLEE SINGERS
BERTRAM D'ARCY, LESLIE RODDA, KENNETH SOLLY,
AND ERIC FAVERSHAM

PRODUCER
H. K. AYLIFF

Scenery designed by PAUL SHELVING

3rd Revival

THE IMMORTAL HOUR

By Rutland Boughton

Presented at the Queen's Theatre on February 9, 1932

Eochaidh	W. JOHNSTONE-DOUGLAS
Etain	GWEN FFRANGCON-DAVIES
Midir	BRUCE FLEGG
Dalua	ARTHUR CRANMER
Manus	APPLETON MOORE
Maive	DOROTHY D'ORSAY
Old Bard	ERIC FORT
Spirit Voice	DOROTHY D'ORSAY

PRODUCER
BARRY JACKSON

CONDUCTOR
ERNEST IRVING

Scenery and costumes designed by PAUL SHELVING

4th Revival

CARAVAN

By Carl Zuckmayer

Produced at the Queen's Theatre on April 6, 1932

Adapted from the German by Cicely Hamilton

Bibbo	MAISIE GAY
Mario	PETER NORTHCOTE
Katherina Kling	EILEEN BELDON
Ignatz Scheel	RICHARD CALDICOT
Julius Schmittolini	O. B. CLARENCE
Lorenz Kling	NORMAN CLARIDGE
Fritz Kling	BARRIE LIVESEY
Karl Kling	CEDRIC HARDWICKE
Membel	WILFRID LAWSON
Martin Rothacker	ROGER LIVESEY
Dillinger	CECIL TROUNCER
Berberitzche	HORACE LYONS
A Farm Labourer	RICHARD MAXWELL
	WILLIAM PRINGLE
	MARGARET CHATWIN
The Eichel Family	VERONICA TESTER
	VERA PEACE
	HARRY UPTON
	MAVIS JONES
Frau Rothacker	DOROTHY HALL
Maali	SALLY

Scenery and costumes by DAME LAURA KNIGHT, A.R.A.

200

HEARTBREAK HOUSE

By Bernard Shaw

Produced at the Queen's Theatre on April 25, 1932

ELLIE DUNN	EILEEN BELDON
NURSE GUINNESS	ISABEL THORNTON
CAPTAIN SHOTOVER	CEDRIC HARDWICKE
LADY UTTERWORD	EDITH EVANS
MRS. HUSHABYE	MARGARET CHATWIN
MAZZINI DUNN	O. B. CLARENCE
HECTOR HUSHABYE	LEON QUARTERMAINE
MANGAN	WILFRID LAWSON
RANDALL UTTERWORD	BALLARD BERKELEY
A BURGLAR	CHARLES GROVES

PRODUCER
H. K. AYLIFF

Scenery designed by PAUL SHELVING

EVENSONG

ADAPTED FROM BEVERLEY NICHOLS' NOVEL

By Edward Knoblock and Beverley Nichols

Produced at the Queen's Theatre on Thursday, June 30, 1932

Scott	TOM WOODS
Tremlowe	BEATRIX FEILDEN-KAYE
Arthur Kober	WILFRID LAWSON
Pauline Lacey	JOAN HARBEN
Irela	EDITH EVANS
Donald Gage	HARRY WILCOXON
John	HOLLAND BENNETT
Julius Rosenberg	REGINALD TATE
Dr. Campbell	DEERING WELLS
Duchess of Rockstone	MARJORIE CHARD
General Sir Ronald Hinchcliffe	DEERING WELLS
Lady Hope Martineau	MOLLIE SHANNON
Capt. Hon. Percy Bragge	BRIAN BUCHEL
Rose Belcher	MARIE SLADE
Mr. Freddie Parks	GERALD CASE
Tom	BOB RUSSELL
1st Elderly Lady	MARGARET CHATWIN
2nd Elderly Lady	ETHEL PERCIVAL
Mr. Stamper	ALBAN BLAKELOCK
Attendant at Opera	HOLLAND BENNETT
Baba L'Étoile	ETHEL GLENDINNING

202

Pablo Sovino	DENNIS VAL-NORTON
Princess Stephanie Rabnitz	VIOLET VANBRUGH
Daphne Carruthers	PAULINE VILDA
Sir Geoffrey Filmer	GUY MARTINEAU
Laura Payne	BARBARA TALLERMAN
Major Dennis Foss	GERALD CASE
Señora de Carranza	NOEL HOOD
Señor de Carranza	COLIN GENT
Señor Luis Moreno	GEORGE DEVINE
Archduke Theodore	FREDERICK LEISTER
Nurse Phillips	LUCY EDWIN

GUESTS

JASMINE BLIGH, CICELY JONAS, DORA BARTON, VIOLET GRAHAM,
EVELYN SPILSBURY, CHRISTINE LINDSAY

PRODUCER
ATHOLE STEWART

Scenery designed by LAURENCE IRVING, *dresses designed by* GILBERT CLARK

203

TOO TRUE TO BE GOOD

By Bernard Shaw

Produced at the New Theatre on September 13, 1932

THE MONSTER	ERNEST THESIGER
THE PATIENT	LEONORA CORBETT
THE ELDERLY LADY	MARGARET HALSTAN
THE DOCTOR	DONALD WOLFIT
THE NURSE	ELLEN POLLOCK
THE BURGLAR	CEDRIC HARDWICKE
COLONEL TALLBOYS, D.S.O.	SCOTT SUNDERLAND
PRIVATE MEEK	WALTER HUDD
SERGEANT FIELDING	RALPH RICHARDSON
THE ELDER	H. K. AYLIFF

PRODUCER
H. K. AYLIFF

The scenery designed by PAUL SHELVING

204

FOR SERVICES RENDERED

By W. Somerset Maugham

Produced at the Globe Theatre on November 1, 1932

LEONARD ARDSLEY	C. V. FRANCE
CHARLOTTE ARDSLEY	LOUISE HAMPTON
SYDNEY	CEDRIC HARDWICKE
EVA	FLORA ROBSON
LOIS	MARJORIE MARS
ETHEL BARTLETT	DIANA HAMILTON
HOWARD BARTLETT	W. CRONIN-WILSON
COLLIE STRATTON	RALPH RICHARDSON
WILFRED CEDAR	S. J. WARMINGTON
GWEN CEDAR	MARDA VANNE
DR. PRENTICE	DAVID HAWTHORNE
GERTRUDE	PHYLLIS SHAND

PRODUCER
H. K. AYLIFF

The scenery designed by PAUL SHELVING

INDEX

INDEX

INDEX